My life is a toilet

My life is a toilet

GRETEL KILLEEN

Random House Australia Pty Ltd
20 Alfred Street, Milsons Point NSW 2061

Sydney New York Toronto
London Auckland Johannesburg
and agencies throughout the world

First published in 1994
Reprinted 1995, 1996, 1997, 1998, 2000 (three times)
Text copyright © Gretel Killeen 1994
Illustrations copyright © 1994

All rights reserved. No part of this publication
may be reproduced, stored in a retrieval system,
or transmitted in any form or by any means,
electronic, mechanical, photocopying, recording
or otherwise, without the prior written permission
of the Publisher.

National Library of Australia
Cataloguing-in-Publication Data

Killeen, Gretel.
  My life is a toilet.

  ISBN 0 09 182850 3.

  1. Title

A823.3

Cover photo by Leslie Solar
Illustrations by Andrew Horn.
Cover design by Luke Atkinson.
Author photograph by Reece Scannell
Typeset by Assett Typesetting, Sydney
Printed by Griffin Press

To Duvavne, (or whatever your name is, your writing is so disgusting it's impossible to read.)

Sorry I took so long to answer, but I didn't feel like it. And basically I just want you to know that I am not at all impressed that you are my new penfriend. Your writing is atrocious and I suspect you are a boy. The only thing good about you is you seem to come from somewhere foreign and exotic, compared to everyone else's penfriends who come from Deniliquin and Wodgoolga. Normally I wouldn't reply to your letter, but I'm feeling fat

AIR MAIL
PAR AVION

24th December
Paradise Island
Wherever that is

and white today so I've decided to become a writer. I will therefore need all the practice I can get, so you're really, really lucky!

from fleur

P.S. Don't think this means I like you or anything.

3rd January
10.29 am

Dear Doodle squat (or whatever your name is),

Hello.
How are you?
How's Paradise Island?
Who cares?

I was thinking about why you didn't write back yet. Then I remembered I think you're a boy.

Boys are so dum. My last boyfriend was so dum it was written all over his face.

And it was spelt wrong.

Anyway, I got a typewriter for Christmas. It's two thousand years old and pretty gross, but better for my writing skills than practising typing on the piano.

Dad gave me the typewriter because I asked him for a word processor. I'm not surprised, one birthday I asked him for some skin products and he gave me a pair of ug boots.

When I first got the typewriter I whinged to Dad that writing on it was absolute agony and all he said was 'That's okay, all good writers have to suffer!' This is pretty typical, and didn't surprise me at all, cause my dad's the type of guy who makes your stomach ache go away by treading really hard on your foot.

Anyway, I can out-suffer the cast of *Days of Our Lives* so if that's all you need to be famous and a huge hit then I'll probably be bigger than Fergie's bottom.

My life is hell!

Sometimes to cheer myself up I sit down and try to think of someone worse off than me.

But I never can.

Anyway enough of Dad, let's talk about me — something everyone says I'm much better at because I practise on the phone all the time.

My name is Fleur. I was named after the head nurse at the maternity hospital where I was born. She was called Fleur de Flem and was a fat and lonely woman. My parents thought *'Fleur'* sounded exotic when I was born, but now it's a 'feminine hygiene' product. This is pretty embarrassing but I guess I should be proud, cause it is the leading brand in Australia.

I live with my mum, her husband and my two loser sisters, Miss Priss and Bum Face, otherwise known as Elizabeth and Kate.

Last year Mum married a guy who looks like the Pope, because when she and Dad split up she converted to Catholicism in a really big way. We're not allowed to call him the Pope of course, so we call him the Pip instead.

The name Pip actually suits him very well because he's small, off white, hard to swallow and hairless.

Dad married his secretary. She's called Babette. It's some sort of European name that means 'she who looks like she has a possum on her head.' Dad was having a fling with her at the office and Mum found out when she popped in to give Dad his sandwiches and found them doing it between the filing cabinet and the tea tray, on which was the tea pot, on which sat the beanie that Mum had knitted for Dad that Father's Day.

Mum was shattered but I wasn't. No, I was just surprised that Mum knew what they were doing.

Anyway she threw Dad out, so he went to Babette's. Then Babette announced she was pregnant. So Dad divorced Mum and married Babette, and Babette gave birth nearly two years later.

And now they're all waiting for me in Dad's Toyota Hi Ace! The whole family, both embarrassing sides, like the fish John West rejects: Dad, the Pip, Mum, the woman with the possum on her head, Miss Priss and Bum Face.

You'll notice Babette didn't bring her baby. That's because she says it'll have much more fun staying with its other grandparents.

Yeah, so would I, and mine are dead.

Normally this situation, of us all being together, just would not be on. My two parents haven't been this close since they got caught together in the whirly doors at the divorce courts when I was eleven.

But now they're waiting in the Hi Ace because we're all driving to Grandma's together.

We have to go in Dad's car with Babette because the Pip's car is still at the mechanics. It's been there since 1978, cause he won't pay the bill. He's like this about a whole lot of useful things, so he spends a heap of time bludging. Mum says the Pip is a God-fearing man. Dad says the Pip is just a tight arse.

Anyway, they're all sitting out in the car and none of them can stand it. I can almost see the fumes of irritation rising from the Hi Ace, just ready to be ignited. All someone has to do is say something incredibly stupid and they could all blow up.

I hope somebody does say something incredibly stupid.

Anyway, we've got to go to Grandma's because she's dying.

I don't care, I never liked her anyway.

I've always hated the way she looks, her thin

skin, her fluffy eyes, her tiny mouth and her stupid perfect plastic teeth.

I hate her laugh, I hate her complaints, I hate her obsession with poppies. I hate the way she tells Elizabeth she's clever, even though I know she only says it cause they're both so dum. And I hate the way she smothers herself in spray on sports deodorant cause it's cheaper than eau de cologne. I hate the way I'm the only person in the world with a grandma who smells like Jeff Fenech.

But I hate her most cause on the day I was born my own grandmother nicknamed me 'Prunehead'.

So anyway I can definitely think of more exciting things to do with my school holidays than go and watch Grandma die. But then again, to tell you the truth, I probably wouldn't be allowed to do them.

I'm only fifteen. But I look much older. Elizabeth's sixteen but acts about three, and Kate's eleven and looks like a jelly blubber.

Mum's like me cause she looks much older too. She reckons she's 40 but she looks 79.

Mum says she used to be really beautiful, but I'm not convinced. I mean *where* is the proof? She just looks a bit like Elvis Presley on his off days now.

My mum should be on *That's Incredible*.

5

When Dad gets drunk he says that Mum is still as beautiful as the day they got married, which probably just means that he always thought she was incredibly ugly.

Mum says beauty on the inside is what really counts, which is the sort of thing people who are really ugly say.

Mum says she was beautiful until we were born. Typical, everything's always my fault. Absolutely everything! But whenever Mum blames me for anything at all I just say, 'Well, I didn't ask to be born!'

This usually makes Mum feel really guilty about sex, so then she shuts up for a while.

The Pip says if God had wanted us to have sex we would have been born in the nude. Once I pointed out that we were born in the nude, and the Pip told me not to be so disgusting. Actually he probably was born wearing clothes: I mean he'd have to have been born wearing something like that mustard terry towelling suit that he's got on now, cause I sure don't think he could have *bought* it anywhere.

Certainly not this century.

What a dag!

He should be on display in a museum, because he's completely stuffed.

Babette and the Pip reckon they can't stand

each other, but I reckon they're secretly in love. The Pip reckons Babette is nothing but a tart, and Babette reckons the Pip's so boring that his mother probably fell asleep giving birth to him.

Oh yuk, I just thought. Imagine being the Pip's mother! Now there's someone worse off than me.

Anyway, I don't think Mum's ever even had sex.

I've got a sneaking suspicion we're adopted.

I hope so.

I'd be so relieved to know that these specimens weren't really my blood relatives.

Anyway, they're all out in the car. Waiting.

10.37am

I can't believe we're going to Grandma's in the school holidays. Why can't she die during term?

I guess I should just try to relax. I'm probably imagining the worst. But I bet we get up there, bored out of our brains, eat too much, put on heaps of weight, kiss her goodbye, get blocked noses from pretending to cry, and then she doesn't drop dead!

I bet she'll make us clean her house and fix

the garden for days and days and then when we've finally finished all her stupid jobs she'll just say she's recovered and send us all back home. That's what she did last time. Mum was so angry she threatened to kill her, but by the time we'd hit on just the right method, Grandma had flown to Club Med.

If she dies this time we'll probably have a party, especially if it's before we do the housework! It'll be great because all the relatives will have to be there and everybody hates each other's guts.

Of course no one hates 'The Pope' (just in case), but Mum hates Dad for obvious reasons, Dad hates Mum for obvious reasons, and we all hate Babette for really obvious reasons. I hate my sisters for obvious reasons, and they hate me for no apparent reason whatsoever. And we all hate Jack, who's Grandma's lover, because the idea is totally disgusting! (Grandma is nearly 92 and he'll be 89 in April.)

They are all ab-sol-ute-ly path-et-ic!

I'd rather be related to the Bee Gees.

And I haven't even mentioned Dildra yet.

Dildra's Dad's sister and she lives in Grandma's house. She hates men and never goes out with them. This makes everyone think she's probably a lesbian, but I just think she's sensible.

(Oh, the Pip thinks a lesbian is someone born in Lebanon, so he doesn't think Dildra's one either.)

Anyway Dildra will be at Grandma's with her best friend Daphne who works in the local library as someone who looks like a librarian.

Dildra and Daphne have been together nineteen years, which is longer than the sum total of all the other relationships in our family, including the ones we don't admit to in public, like sisters et cet er a.

Nobody ever thought it would last because Dildra's always going through phases. Last year she did macrame, pottery, watercolours *and* boot making, while she was sitting in a small plastic pyramid in the middle of her living room.

At the moment she's learning Japanese by correspondence. Grandma doesn't care because she's deaf, but she worries that if Jack hears Japanese spoken in the house it might set him off on a World War 2 flashback and then he'll try to kill Dildra. What Grandma doesn't realise is that Jack won't hear because he's deaf too. She just thinks he's incredibly rude.

I hope Jack does waste Dildra. Especially while we're there. But he probably won't.

Because nothing exciting ever happens on our holidays.

One Easter Babette swallowed a bluebottle, turned purple and nearly died. That was pretty funny, absolutely hilarious. But she's been really boring ever since.

I tell you, sometimes I wonder if I'm the only one alive in this place. Or maybe *I'm* dead and this is hell.

Anyway, so they'll both be at Grandma's, Dildra and Daphne, wearing matching floral print dresses, skull cap hairdoes and soft padded shoes, dressed as total dags. Actually the best thing about seeing Dildra and Daphne is that no matter what you happen to be wearing they always make you feel really fashionable.

Normally we only see them when they come down to Sydney to do something like buy new elastic for their cotton tails. They do this about every five years, and I think they do it too often.

I actually like Dildra and Daphne, but Dad goes really weird when they're around because Dad doesn't like Dildra and Dildra doesn't like Dad.

Dad says Dildra wants Grandma's money. Dildra says Dad wants Grandma's house. Dad says Dildra needs to get herself a man. Dildra looks at Dad and says she'd rather just get rid of one.

Mum seems to side a bit with Dildra on this issue. But I think that's only because she relates to Dildra as another woman who doesn't have sex with men.

No one would have sex with the Pip. He's about as sexually attractive as mould. Where some men stick socks down the front of their pants, he looks like he sticks pillows down the back.

Actually I'm exaggerating completely, cause he really only looks exactly like a two legged sock that's been soaking in algae.

Well all right maybe he doesn't look like that, but that's exactly how he makes you feel.

To tell you the truth all my relatives look a bit weird. It's really quite amazing I don't.

Dad looks like Dustin Hoffman when he was Tootsie.

Mum looks like Julia Roberts in the dark.

Elizabeth looks just like Miss Piggy. And you can't take Kate to the zoo in case one of the gorillas wants to marry her.

Babette looks okay from a really long way away, but it's expensive to fly to New Zealand.

(I wish Tom Cruise and Nicole would adopt me. Actually I wish just Tom would.)

Aaaaaaaaaanyway, where was I? Oh yeah the Pip. Well he's never met Grandma before in his life but he's coming along to give Mum support. Why Mum is going to Grandma's is a mystery to everyone cause we all know they hate each other's guts. Grandma hates Mum because she divorced Dad, and Mum hates Grandma because she gave birth to him.

Anyway, I've got a sneaking suspicion Mum wants to convert Grandma to Catholicism while she's kicking the bucket, and is too weak to tell Mum to get lost. Religious people try to do this sort of thing all the time, I think it's cause basically they're all really scared that when they finally do actually get to heaven they'll be the only ones up there.

Dad says he couldn't care less about God, but he wants to see Grandma before she dies because that's the sort of thing a son should do. And besides Babette wants first claim on the book case in Grandma's hallway.

10.45 am

They're still waiting for me to join them in the Hi Ace, but I'm just sitting here in my bedroom squeezing a blackhead on my nose.

See, what none of them seems to realise is that when I say I'm not coming out and getting into the car I mean I'm never leaving this house again! It's not my fault, it's all my mum's, cause she's the one who trimmed my hair this morning and now I look like someone whipper-snipped my head!

You always know your hair cut is a disaster when your mum finishes and tells you 'it'll grow'.

Well if it is going to grow, they can just sit there till it does.

10.47 am

Oh great. Now the whole van's bouncing up and down, so people from a distance will think someone's 'doing it' inside.

As if. The van's only bouncing cause when Dad's annoyed he jiggles. Honestly, the last time anyone did anything dirty in one of Dad's cars was when Elizabeth got car sick and vomited.

10.48 am

Now Dad's saying, 'Come on, Fleur, hurry up!' and everyone else is joining in the chorus, like a plague of seagulls on Bondi Beach squawking for your last hot chip.

I'm ignoring them as much as I can by doing my impression of Helen Keller.

10.52 am

The bomb Hi Ace that they're all sitting in belongs to my father and it's so disgusting it makes facial bum fluff look attractive. It's the most off colour and it's got no air conditioning which is absolutely typical cause my father is as tight as size 6 undies.

Molto embarrassanto!

I know you're probably thinking 'Sure, the fact that your car is the colour of pooh is embarrassing, and the fact that your parents drive it with the protective plastic still covering the seats so that when it gets really, really hot the plastic melts and sticks to your legs, yeah that's embarrassing, especially when you realise that it's also exactly the same car as retirement villages use when they're driving their gerries to lawn bowls competitions! Yeah that's embarrassing. That is embarrassing! But no air conditioning,' I bet you think, 'I don't think so!'

Well it is embarrassing when you have to sit in the car with your face going bright red and your dad drives with his arm out the window and ends up with a big sunburned sleeve stripe that everyone sees when you go to the beach so they know you don't have air conditioning and your relatives are poor and that your mother probably made the sack bikini that you're wearing, and obviously gave you that hair trim!

It's soooooooooo embarrassing having scrooge parents; all my friends feel completely sorry for me and reckon it'd be heaps more socially acceptable if my dad was in jail.

See both my parents find it impossible to spend money. (Which is another reason why I think I'm adopted) for Christmases and birthdays they just give each other IOU's. Dad can't buy anything unless it's an absolute necessity and Mum can't buy anything unless it's half price, which means the thing's either broken or bad or so incredibly disgusting that no one else in the known world wants it.

You can imagine how well we're all dressed.

Basically as far as I'm concerned life's embarrassing, and then you die.

10.54 am

Well writing all that took one and a half minutes. What a complete waste of time, nothing achieved, nothing changed, absolutely nothing learned. I could have fallen in love in half that time, then agonised about it for the rest of my life!

They're still waiting in the car.

My little sister, Kate Bottom Nose is going bright red. Now everyone will know about the air conditioning.

Told you!

My older sister, Elizabeth the worm face, is crawling to Mum by pointing out all the bits of lawn that the Pip missed with the new cordless wonder blade mower that he borrowed from Dad.

Dad hates lending the Pip anything, because Dad really hates the Pip. Mum reckons it's just cause Dad's jealous, but I reckon jealous of what?

Anyway, the first time the Pip asked how you start the wonder mower, Dad told him you had to lie under it.

Babette gave Dad the wonder mower for Christmas. They're a really romantic couple.

Dad gave Babette a box of chocolates, which is pretty cruel considering she weighs about four million kilos in the shade.

10.56 am

Oh vom villia!

They're still waiting in the car.

Dad's arm is going stripey.

Mum's starting to knit.

Mum knits absolutely all the time, which of course is another reason why I think she must be seventy. Only old people knit. And it's really embarrassing. No one else's mother knits for their family: at worst they just threaten to if the kids are really bad.

But Mum knits all the time. It's an obsession. If she didn't knit she'd probably either weigh 4 million kilos like Babette, or be a heroin addict. Some people have just got addictive personalities.

Apparently it's genetically inherited.

Oh no!

Now I've depressed myself again.

My eldest sister, Elizabeth the snot ear, actually *encourages* Mum to knit. I tell you Elizabeth would wear my mother's tuna casserole on her head if she thought it would make Mum happy.

What an idiot! Doesn't she realise that nothing makes Mum happy, beeeeeeeecause nothing's supposed to? She's a mother for heaven's sake. She's meant to suffer and be depressed.

That's why she couldn't be complete without me.

11.05 am

They're still out in the car.

Mum and Dad'll probably start fighting soon.

If someone was watching all this they'd say I'd made my parents unbearably tired and irritable. But actually they've always been like that.

Sometimes I wish my parents would abandon me in a cardboard box somewhere.

Sometimes?

Make that every minute of every day that I've ever been alive.

Actually ever since I was born I wanted my parents to get divorced. Because all my friends whose parents were divorced got really great presents for Christmas and their birthdays. So what happened? My parents got divorced and all my friends still get much better presents than me for Christmas and their birthdays and I just get twice as many really dum ones.

Adoption is the only way.

I used to have this theory that I was swapped at birth with Princess Caroline of Monaco. No one ever believed me, probably cause I made the stupid mistake of choosing someone to be swapped at birth with who was twenty years older than me.

I wish I could say a bit more in French, then I'd write something poetic right now. But all I can say is 'where is the cat?'

'Under the table thanks, Madam.'

Oh well.

Ou est le chat?

BUM.

11.07 am

Well they're *still* waiting and I'm still in my bedroom, watching them through the cigarette burn hole I made in my curtain the time I smoked out my window to impress the neighbour's gardener, whom I find quite attractive when I'm desperate. But it was pretty unimpressive cause I set off our house smoke detectors and had a stress-induced asthma attack.

Anyway, I'm still in my room and I know Babette's about to break another diet because I can see her secretly struggling to open her Christmas chocolates out of the side window of the Hi Ace. This is not a good sign! I'll probably have to go out to the car pretty soon, otherwise Dad'll get so hugely annoyed he'll make us listen to the cricket all the way to Grandma's.

Oh well, I guess I've proved my point now anyway. I've kept them waiting for nearly forty-five minutes, and I'm sure my hair must have grown at least a bit.

11.12 am

I'm in the Hi Ace now. And no one's talking to me. They all think this is a terrible punishment but I'm actually thrilled to bits.

I'd describe the scenery in here but I can't see the point because what's inside the Hi Ace is even more boring than what you can find on the outside. It's a bit like those cheap assorted chocolates.

But basically the interior is beige with big pink blops.

The beige is the seats, the ceiling and the floor and the blops are all my relatives.

11.13 am

I'm sitting between Elizabeth the crawler and Katie the sulk. Katie, my younger sister, sulks all the time, because that way she gets whatever she wants. Everyone tells her she's really, really pretty but I tell her that her face looks like it was run over by a steam roller.

I wish someone would tell me I was pretty. Someone other than Dave Simmons who lives down the road and looks like a piece of used dental floss. I've known him since I was about nought years old and he still thinks he wants to marry me.

Once he kissed me and I nearly vomited.

I guess if I married him I'd stay pretty skinny because he really puts me off my food.

11.45 am

Well, we've been sitting in the van now for about half an hour but Dad drives so slowly we're only two blocks from home.

They reckon you can tell a lot about a man by the car that he drives. Well this car looks like dog-do on wheels.

Dad says he drives slowly to avoid the police but we've already been stopped by them three times this morning because when they see anyone driving this slow they assume he must be doing something illegal.

As if. The naughtiest thing my dad's ever done is blow a raspberry once when Grandma sat down. He was eleven at the time, and you probably remember she's deaf.

But Mum drives even worse than Dad, with one foot on the accelerator, one foot on the brake, one hand on the steering wheel and one hand waving out the window while she screams, 'Quick, get out of the way!'

I hate to think how Mum actually got her licence. If she was better looking I'd have to suggest that she'd offered the examiner sex if she passed. But in the case of my mother I'd suggest she *threatened* sex if he *didn't* let her pass.

Em barras sing. (That's Latin for 'to be so overwhelmingly embarrassed you're worried your face might get stretch marks'.)

12.34 pm

Well we're still in the shamemobile. But now we're not moving at all. We haven't even been driving for an hour yet and Mum and Dad and Babette and the Pip have all decided they need a cup of tea. Good God.

The Pip says he can't breathe without a cup of tea, so I suggest we keep on driving.

12.35 pm

So now we've stopped by the side of the road to perform the *Trotter tea ceremony*. And I wish I could fall unconscious at will. Or else turn my family into pot plants.

We've parked in a ditch because the Pip directed Dad while he reversed, and the Pip wasn't wearing his glasses. He's too vain to wear them in public, but personally I think he looks much better with at least part of his face covered up.

Anyway so we're parked in the most public position possible, where everyone I've ever known in my life can drive past and perv. I should have known my life was going to be embarrassing from the first moment that I was born, when I saw my ugly father's face and hoped I'd got out at the wrong stop.

12.36 pm

Now they're getting out a tartan rug, but before they put it on the ground, I guarantee they'll do a 'pooh patrol'.

Doing a 'pooh patrol' is probably the closest thing to living death caused by embarrassment that anyone could ever experience. What you have to do is walk round peering at the ground, armed with a long thick stick. Then when you see an animal pooh you yell 'There's one!' and flick it like a golf ball into the bush.

But this time I'm not getting out of the van. They can pooh patrol to their heart's content but I'm sitting right here. I'm just going to sit here and concentrate on growing my hair.

I don't care if they pooh patrol by themselves. It'll do them good. What they all need is to feel alone, desperately humiliated, stupid and ridiculous. The way they make me feel all the time.

12.40 pm

I'm still in the van, all alone except for my two loser sisters who are asleep like slugs.

12.42 pm

They're still doing 'pooh patrol'.

Because I'm in the Hi Ace I'm much higher than the patrollers and I can look down and spit on the Pip's bald patch. Unfortunately I keep missing, but if I hit the bull's eye I'm going to yell, 'Hey there's a bird poop on your head!' And then someone might flick him like a golf ball into the bush.

And if all that happens then this will definitely go down as the most exciting family holiday to date.

12.47 pm

Well now they've finished their patrol and they've found a poohless patch to safely lay out the dag tartan picnic rug. It's actually really too small to be called a rug. Mum knitted it as a poncho for the dog. But the dog's dead now, so it doesn't need it. He was a chihuahua that everyone hated, cause he was just like a rat that barked. We didn't treat him with hate of course, we just fed him *Like* dogfood instead of *Luv*.

We pretended to love him, we fed him, watered him and ignored him (like you do with the rest of the family) but then one day he was riding in the basket on the front of my bicycle just outside our house when I hit a bump and he just flew off. We honestly couldn't find him anywhere at all, but it's interesting that our chimney's been blocked ever since.

But don't tell Kate. Cause it was her dog. And she'll take it really personally cause she's a sulk and she'll just act like we wished we'd stuck her in the chimney. (Actually that's given me an idea.)

Anyway, Babette's pouring boiling water from the tartan thermos into the matching plastic cups. Dad's extracting the used tea bags with two spoons, then carrying the bags squished between the spoons, at arm's length, over to the bin. People always carry used tea bags like this, like they're afraid the bags might be carriers of some gross contagious disease. Poor little tea bags, as if they'd carry diseases. It's far more likely Dad is.

Meanwhile, my mother's blowing really hard on her home made devon sandwiches. She left them in the freezer too long last night and now she's trying to defrost them.

It's dangerous to eat frozen devon sandwiches you know because the icicles can get caught in your throat. But Mum makes us eat things like this all the time. We all have very comprehensive life insurance.

Anyway, I'm still in the Hi Ace and now I can see Dad's trying to saw the sandwiches into quarters using the fingernail cleaning blade on his Swiss army knife.

Actually it's not really a Swiss army knife.

Dad would never be so extravagant. It's a cheap imitation that he bought on sale from the back of someone's truck and Swiss is spelt with five 'esses'.

12.48 pm

Things were looking promising with the sandwich until the blade snapped off the Swisssss army knife and now Babette's starting to yell at Mum about how stupid Mum's sandwiches are.

12.49 pm

Mum just chucked a sandwich at Babette's head and knocked her out cold.

So now Babette doesn't have a clue about anything that's going on around her. And I'm almost envious.

12.50 pm

Dad's trying to get Babette back to normal. (Yeh good luck). And the Pip is passing the killer sandwiches round. He secretly separated them with a chisel and hammer he found in the boot, and then rested them on the hot exhaust pipe to defrost while he revved the engine.

So now we're all gagging on Mum's melted sandwiches. They taste a bit wet, they look a little black and I think if we sniffed them we'd probably hallucinate.

12.51 pm

Well Babette is lying perfectly still, she's either dead, or paralysed or really bunging it on and just enjoying the attention. I think she probably thinks that she looks very dramatic, but lying there dressed in her emerald green kaftan she just looks like a fat zucchini with a possum on its head.

Actually I think it's getting pretty obvious that Babette needs mouth to mouth resuscitation, but no one's willing to give it to her. Mum says she'll give me five bucks to revive her, we settle on eleven, so I'll do it.

Sometimes I wish I'd never done first aid at school, but then I never would have had an excuse to kiss my teacher, Mr Bringley, during practice.

Of course there was probably no excuse for the way I wrapped my legs around him and yelled 'Do it to me baby, I'm yours!'

12.54 pm

Anyway, Babette's starting to moan like some sort of porno starlet and Dad's covered her head with a blanket to try to muffle the noise. She's struggling to take it off because it's hard to breathe, but she looks much better with it on.

Oh, by the way, I'm outside the van now. I had to leave the safety of the Hi Ace because Mum wanted me to save Babette's life. So now I'm standing with my head between my legs so that only someone tunnelling and emerging at my feet could have any chance at all of recognising me.

But I'm wearing Dad's sunglasses and Mum's floppy straw hat anyway, just as an extra precaution. Right now I could be anyone else in the world.

I wish I was.

12.58 pm

In a position like this everyone thinks I'm going to vomit, so they're leaving me alone.

I should stand like this all the time.

12.60 pm

Well Dad's trying to get Babette into the van but she's lying completely stiff and doing this sort of insurance claim act where she complains about her neck, her legs, her arms and her back. Personally I reckon she's carrying it all a bit far, considering Mum only clipped the tip of her hairdo, but Dad's treating Babette like she's precious anyway. He must have been hit on the head too. Obviously this is a rare occasion so who can blame her for making the most of it?

Me.

I find this whole situation absolutely pathetic. To pretend that you're dead and ask for lots of attention is immature, shameful and beneath contempt.

I wish I'd thought of it first.

I used to pretend to be dead quite a lot. But I did it so often that it reached the point where Mum just vacuumed the house around me.

Last year I fainted when I got out of the shower, and that was dramatic, but then my towel fell off and everyone saw me nude and I nearly fell into an embarrassment coma! Of course where *you* live on Paradise Island you probably run around in the nuddy all the time, but you have to understand that I'm entering that difficult stage in any woman's life, where I feel slightly uncomfortable with my own body. Apparently it'll last from now until about the day that I die.

1.02 pm

Well during the past little while not much has happened. Babette fainted again for no reason at all. Then she came to when I stuck two mothballs up her nostrils, and then she took one look at Dad's ugly face and immediately passed out again.

This is really bad. Now she's going to have to travel horizontally and the only way she can do that is if they lay her down across the back seat on our laps. But it's too sticky-hot to do something stupid like this and besides she won't fit, so we're going to poke her feet out the side window of the van and drive like that for a while instead.

1.04 pm

We're not driving like that anymore because an Aussie Tours bus came too close and took off with one of Babette's sandals.

1.05 pm

Now we've just sort of bent her so her legs fold under the middle seat. I hope the wind changes cause if she gets stuck in this position, I can use her as a foot stool.

1.08 pm

Okay, now I'm really squashed because the unconscious fat Babette has shifted one foot to rest underneath my chin. It's hard to write and impossible to breathe. I'm going to suggest we move Babette onto the floor, and lay her in the space between the seats and the door.

1.09 pm

Well, I suggested it.

Dad said we can't do that because someone might tread on her.

So Mum's decided it's a very good idea.

1.11 pm

So now Babette's lying on the floor of the Hi

Ace and we've wedged an esky on each side of her, between her shoulders and the car seats. We've basically done this to stop her rolling all over the place, and because it looks really funny.

1.27 pm

I'm going to get bored soon.
    What'll I do?
    Moan a bit.
    That usually gets a good response.

1.29 pm

Mum told me to shut up.
    I think I'll just breathe really loud for a while and stick my foot into Elizabeth salami head's big fat bum.

1.31 pm

Okay, that took about nought seconds.
    Only 7 hours, 43 minutes and 50 seconds to go till we get to Grandma's. Make that 49 seconds, no 48 seconds, no 47, 46, 45, 44, 43, 42 ...

I haven't been this bored and depressed since the day I was born.

1.37 pm

Oh.

This trip is taking forever.

Why does Grandma have to live in Curlewis? Or more to the point, why does she have to go and die there!

Curlewis is more than a million k's from anything useful or even vaguely attractive. And what's more Grandma lives on a farm, which is pretty embarrassing, considering farms went out of fashion about ten years before the Beach Boys.

Grandma says she likes the wide open spaces and clean fresh air. And I say yes, but where are the shopping malls?

And where's the air conditioning!?

Maybe Grandma's just gone mad and doesn't realise that she lives in the boon docks with an 89 year old pervert. Maybe I should tell her when we arrive. I'll be gentle of course, cause I don't want her to cark it before she's converted, so I'll just say, 'Grandma, what the hell are you doing wasting your life away in this hole?'

And she'll say, 'Hole? I thought I was happily

ensconced in an inner city air conditioned high rise, close to all the very best bars and of course the best dance clubs!'

And I'll say, 'WRONG!'

And she'll say, 'Take me where the action is.'

And I'll say, 'Yeah, baby, come on let's go!'

And then I'll ask Dad to give us a lift.

Dum de dum.

1.38 pm

Actually the view is quite nice out the side window of the dagmobile Hi Ace. I like watching the bugs smash against the glass and just stick in their own goop until they're blown off and onto the road where they're immediately run over by a truck.

1.39 pm

Now I think I'll pretend to be asleep.

1.40 pm

Okay I did that. It wasn't much fun or

particularly exciting, so I'm awake again now.

Half of my rels are fast asleep and the other are fully conscious, but it's hard to tell which are which.

1.41 pm

We're about to overtake some guy with a bicycle. At last a sign of life!

This is great, I love boys!

Maybe we'll get married and he can help me escape the rels. I hope he's good looking and incredibly wealthy.

I know all this makes me sound pretty desperate, but the truth is I'd marry his bicycle.

He's stopped by the side of the road to patch a tyre. If he hadn't stopped we couldn't overtake him, because at the speed that Dad travels we can only overtake objects that are either stationary or dead.

Well, I reckon with this guy in the gutter unable to escape now's the perfect time to try my new boy tactics. Usually I play hard to get with guys. In fact if I absolutely adore one I just ignore him completely. Thing is this is exactly what I do to boys I reckon are absolutely gross, so you can imagine I don't score very often.

But anyway, now I've completely changed and I'm not going to be shy and subtle like that any more. See I had a religious experience during sex education and realised that if I keep on like this I'll have the sex life of a nun.

So when we pass this guy I'm going to point at my cleavage and squash it against the window. (I have to point at my cleavage in case he can't see it, which is what happened with the lady when I got my last bra fitted.)

1.42 pm

Okay, I did that and it hurt quite a bit!

Why did I do it? I'm a moron!

Now I've probably done irreversible damage. Now my boobs'll probably never grow . . . or worse, just start popping out my back!

Oh well it may have been painful and embarrassing but it's all over now and I survived and I know I'll never see the guy or his bicycle ever again. That's a relief. After the time I jumped on Mr Bringley and said 'Do it to me, baby, I'm yours', he ended up teaching me for three years in a row.

1.45 pm

Oh no, gross suffering!

Dad's stopped the Hi Ace and he says he's thinking of reversing.

All the way back to the cyclist!

Mum's making him do it.

Funny how Dad still does what Mum tells him even though he pretends he can't hear her.

Mum says this guy might be injured or need help in some way. But Dad says we shouldn't reverse and pick him up because the cyclist might be a pervert. He says that the cyclist might kill the men and kidnap the women.

So, I selflessly abandon my tres embarrassment and vote we go back and get him immediately.

1.46 pm

As we get closer to the cyclist it's becoming really obvious that he and his bicycle are perfectly all right. Until Dad runs over them both while he's reversing.

1.46 and a half pm

Things are looking pretty bad, even uglier than

the time I saw Dave Simmons's tonsils when I caught him practising a tongue kiss on his mother's front windscreen.

Now things are looking unbelievably bad cause the cyclist is wearing those obscenely tight bike shorts and from the waist to the thighs (and the bits in between) he looks like a tightly wrapped meat tray.

1.47 pm

Oh vomit. He's standing up and walking towards us. I hope he doesn't make himself infertile by taking too big a step in those shorts.

I'm not actually going to look at him walk because it might make me car sick.

1.51 pm

Now stupid Mum's offering him a lift. And the seat next to me!

This is absolutely typical. I just hope his bike shorts aren't catching.

1.53 pm

I'm holding my *Golly* magazine over my face

cause I'm trying to hide from this creep. He's trying to talk to me so I've written a sign with a picture of a nutcracker that says SPEAK AND YOU'LL REGRET IT.

Why is it that the only guys who ever pay me any attention are the ones who are sort of mutated. Where are the strong, intelligent, interesting people? All born as girls I suspect.

I always get very depressed about my boy situation. Then I talk to Mum. Then Mum gets very very depressed and says 'what are you so depressed about, you're single, you're free, why can't you accept that this is the best time of your life?' And then I get really depressed.

Then she always says 'plenty more fish in the sea' and I say 'yeah, mullets and gropers'.

1.54 pm

Now we're driving again. Through the country. Great big flocks of sheep ... both outside and inside the van.

Plop-face, the cyclist, is talking to Dad about accounting variables. They're both laughing away, having a great time, getting on like a house on fire and really enjoying each other's company.

The guy *must* be a drop kick.

Mum'll probably marry him next.

1.57 pm

Major depression.

1.59 pm

Oh no, the van just tilted really badly.

I think we've hit a severe pot hole.

Great, another bit of symbolism for my life.

I reckon the reason for *this* crisis is the bike bloke's endless blab about accounting which has put everyone in the van to sleep, including Dad who's driving.

2 pm

Okay, so we've stopped the Hi Ace *again*.

I tell you this trip is more frustrating than trying to wee in a bodysuit.

2.02 pm

The car won't start cause its front wheel is sort of stuck and the load is too heavy to get it out.

I suggested we could lighten the load if we threw Elizabeth out the window.

And Elizabeth told me to 'shut up'.

Yeah, good come-back, balloon bum!

Now Mum just said that if I don't 'stop being silly' she's going to throw me out the window. Good, I reckon. Throw me out the window, run me over with the Hi Ace, stick your knitting needles in my ears, see if I care, none of it could possibly be any worse than sitting in the Hi Ace with your relatives!

2.02 *and a bit pm*

I'm trying to cheer myself up by thinking of a time when I was carefree and happy.

2.02 *and a half pm*

I can't think of one.

2.02 *and three quarters pm*

The men've decided to 'get out and have a look'. This is an Australian term, whatever your name is, that means the men will get out, and look at the car, while some loser wife or exploited daughter who doesn't get nearly enough love, attention or pocket money, walks two thousand kilometres to call the local road service.

Men are useless. The only thing they're really good for is filling y-front undies.

2.02 *but nearly 2.03 pm*

Anyway, all this 'get out and have a look stuff' means we're going to be stopped by the side of the road again. I tell you, if Mum brings out the thermos I'll die.

She brought out the thermos.

THE END.

Only joking.

2.03 pm

Well we don't need to call the road service after all because as soon as the fat toad Pip and the snot-moustached-Dad got out of the Hi Ace to do their have a look thing the van was light enough to roll out of the pot hole without them. Pity it didn't keep rolling.

My life has been a series of lost opportunities, it started when I wasn't swapped mysteriously at birth.

Or maybe I was and that's the problem.

Hey, that's good, I've cheered myself up now. But I won't let it show! It's seriously against my religion. Our family motto is 'no pain no gain' and we rigorously apply it to everything in life: food and clothing and interior design.

2.07 pm

Everyone's back in the Hi Ace now. Kate and Elizabeth are discussing the lyrics to *Feelin' Groovy* and agreeing they don't know what they mean, Babette's trying to scrape the old chocolate from under her fingernails, and the Pip's trying to get something disgusting out of his ear. I hope he doesn't pull out his brain.

I've got nothing to do. Just sit here being bored. I think I'll daydream about Warwick Paston. I love him so I'll dream the usual that he's in love with me, we get married, become huge social celebs, entertain beautiful people who are absolutely loaded, wear lavish clothes and buy expensive property and laugh and smile and are in all the mags until Warwick dies in a hideous highly publicised jet crash, and leaves all his money to me.

Maybe I don't love him that much after all.

2.09 pm

Now Mum's busy thanking God for getting us out of the pot hole. Of course it doesn't seem to occur to her to blame him for putting us there in the first place!

I wish Mum would go back to sleep, that way I could either pretend she doesn't exist or else sort of psych flies to land in her mouth.

Actually you shouldn't say things like that about your mother. It's safer just to think them. If there's one thing I've learnt in my short agonised life, it's never say anything rude to your mother, if there's any way she could possibly hear you.

But parents can say whatever they want. Like they don't say 'Fleur, get that knife out of the toaster, you might get electrocuted and that would be a tragedy because we love you so much.' No they say, 'Fleur, you'll break the toaster doing that.' Like they're really disappointed when you don't cark it and just ruin their one chance of freedom.

I tell you, the only reason I stick around is to get back at Mum and Dad. They had me; let them suffer.

Of course I've thought of death, who hasn't! Not *my* death of course, just everybody else's — like Mum and Dad's and Elizabeth's and Kate's and the Pip's and Babette's and ...

2.12 pm

Now Mum's decided that Dad should have a rest, and because Babette's still unconscious on the floor and the Pip is pathetic, Mum's decided to drive. This'll be good! She'll probably forget to take the Hi Ace out of reverse and we'll end up further away from Grandma's than we were when we started off this morning.

Good.

2.20 pm

Well she didn't forget to take it out of reverse, but she did make us all get out of the van while she steered it around the pot hole. She said she needed space to concentrate.

Yeah, like the one between her ears wasn't enough.

I mean if Mum can't even start the engine with all of us in the van, how I ask you is she going to drive us all anywhere? Pretty badly I guess.

But anyway, we're back in the Hi Ace again.

Unfortunately.

Now that Mum's driving, Dad's sitting in the front passenger seat pretending he isn't here. He's wearing a sleeping mask with a really cheap pair of imitation Ray-Bans over the top (the sort you buy at petrol stations or get free with every two dozen cokes). The glasses have an arm missing so they're sitting on his face lop-sided. Whenever I talk to him and he's wearing these glasses I always subconsciously lean the other way, to try to make up the difference.

Actually that part is a little exaggerated, cause I never try to talk to Dad.

Anyway, he's stuck one of those stupid travelling pillows over his head and he's listening to the cricket on dead Grandpa's hearing aid. It somehow works as a radio if you stick a coat hanger in the top and make sure your nose is pointing north east.

Mum's singing 'Onward Christian Soldiers' at the top of her terrible voice, not because it brings joy to anyone, but because she knows it pisses Dad off.

Sometimes I wish Mum and Dad would get back together. I mean if they had each other to constantly get annoyed with, it would sure take the pressure off me.

I personally am never going to get married. It's unnatural to be committed to just one person for the rest of your life, and besides marriage seems to make your bum spread.

2.24 pm

Now stupid Elizabeth's started singing harmonies with Mum, because she is, as I said, a supreme crawler. God I think she's annoying! How can I make her go away?

Once I pretended I wanted to practise my first aid bandages, and tied her to a chair in the back yard and left her there. Now that was hilarious, till Dad found out and got really angry cause the bandages scratched the chair's paint job.

Basically Elizabeth should be left alone in a cage and occasionally fed bananas. I should get Mum to suggest this to her, cause then Elizabeth'd probably do it.

I tell you, I just have to be adopted.

2.25 pm

Great, Elizabeth just passed out. I guess she must have suddenly realised exactly how stupid she is. And that took her breath away. And now she's unconscious.

The cyclist, who by the way is still sitting next to me with his tightly wrapped lunch in his shorts, is *still* talking! I've got my fingers stuck in my ears and nearly everyone other than loser Mum is asleep, so Mum's forced to listen to him.

2.26 pm

Dad's just made me take my fingers out of my ears. Apparently I was affecting his reception.

2.27 pm

I think the cyclist just said that he thinks God is an extinct phenomenon designed to justify the agony of existence.

2.28 pm

Mum's starting to sing a bit flat.

2.29 pm

Now the cyclist's saying that God was created to deceive the masses into accepting a life of subservience and frustration, and to delude men and women into thinking that they could one day be rewarded for their uselessness.

2.30 pm

Mum seems a bit distracted. Her face is going blue and the Hi Ace is kangaroo jumping down the expressway.

2.30 and a half pm

I just called out 'Change gear!' and Elizabeth came to and said, 'Why, what's wrong with what Mum's wearing?'

2.31 pm

Now the cyclist is saying that anyone who believes in God is shallow and escapist. He's saying that anyone who worships God is a desperate blinded thoughtless fool looking for a quick fix answer. He's saying they'd do better selling pens for the poor outside a suburban shopping mall than merely sustaining an archaic institution based on fallacy and fraud. He's saying that people who devote their lives to God may as well kill themselves right here and now because this life is all there is, and it doesn't get any better.

2.32 pm

Mum just drove the front of the Hi Ace into the back of the ute in front.

2.34 pm

Well, they've stopped so we've stopped. I think this is absolutely stupid. What's the point in standing here and taking all the blame. I reckon we should have just done a hit and run. Why not? I do it to my sisters all the time.

Anyway, I guess now is as good a time as ever to go and wee in the bush.

2.35 pm

I'm looking for the perfect spot. I've been

waiting three and a half hours to do this wee and there's no way I'm settling for second best. Of course I settle for third best, fourth best or even worse in most other aspects of my life so why I draw the line at this I don't know ... probably cause you can control your wee, and boyfriends you just can't.

It's ridiculous that I need to wee now — in the bush. We were only at one of those super dooper 'clean and go' petrol stations not that long ago, but I was thinking about other things at the time. I was thinking about the time the tight arse Pip borrowed Dad's car and spent the whole night stealing petrol from the neighbours. And how, while he was trying to suck it out of their petrol tanks with a hose, he swallowed so much he ended up in hospital for thirteen days. And for nearly a whole year after that wasn't allowed to go near naked flames, smokers or farters.

Anyway, back to the wee.

Doesn't it always happen that way, that you never feel the need to 'go' at the petrol station, but always, as soon as you're on the expressway, past the sign that says NO STOPPING, NO TURNING BACK you just become desperate.

2.36 pm

I'm standing in the middle of the bush now looking round, with my legs crossed.

I feel like a clothes peg.

Anyway. Where was I, oh, yes, the wee. Which I really should have typed in upper case bold italics, because it's all become so important now. So, **THE WEE.**

I tell you, it's times like these, weeing in the bush that you know God is totally sexist.

2.38 pm

Okay, that was relatively painless except that I wee'd a little bit on my shoe and I've got a gum leaf stuck on my bum.

2.43 pm

I'm back at the van. Mum's standing next to the front door squeaking like a rat and Dad's still got a pillow on his head.

The Pip said, 'There, there, give me a cuddle,' and Mum told him not to be so disgusting.

Then Dad told the Pip to sit abruptly on a frozen devon sandwich and Mum looked at

Dad the way she used to when she loved him, which was a long time before I was born. And then Dad said to the Pip, 'Look what's happened to my pride and joy!' And Mum stupidly thought he was talking about her but he was really just talking about his Hi Ace. Meanwhile Babette's snoring. She's not asleep; she's just snoring cause that's the way she breathes. But the slugs are asleep. Not even the thrill of a near death experience has managed to wake them up. I shouldn't criticise them. It probably takes a lot of energy to be completely plop heads *all* the time.

2.45 pm

Babette's trying to force the cyclist to tell her that her hair looks 'bootiful'. Of course he won't unless he's blind, but she's speaking to him in German because she thinks it sounds more authoritative.

2.46 pm

The cyclist is trying to confuse Babette by talking to her in a special language that he's made up himself, where you just say every word backwards. But what the stupid cyclist doesn't realise is that Babette understands every word that he's saying because she *thinks* backwards anyway.

I think he's telling her something about nett cashflow and depreciation funding in an annual broadsheet accounting ledger pre tax performance.

Ordinarily this sort of line would make anyone want to vomit, but it's actually the line Dad first used to *seduce* Babette. I know because I heard it. They were in Dad's office and I was under his desk doing work experience at the time, snoozing.

(Sleeping on the job is absolutely the only benefit to having a father's who's head of an accounting department.)

Guys and their pick up lines. Once this guy asked me if I'd talk to him because he'd just lost his house. I said 'oh no, was it flood, fire, a brutal storm?' And he said no: he just couldn't find it.

2.51 pm

Babette has just grabbed the cyclist and she's saying, 'Do it to me, bud. Let me handle your credit column.'

2.52 pm

Now the cyclist is saying 'on' (which translated means 'no'.)

2.52 and a half pm

Babette's punching his tightly wrapped liverwurst.

2.53 pm

Ha, now I'm watching the cyclist escape on what used to be his bicycle, just the back wheel, the luggage rack and one lonely stupid pedal, all by itself. It's clumsy and uncomfortable and reminds me of Dad.

At the moment it looks like he can only cycle in circles but if he makes them wide enough he should reach Bourke by Thursday.

2.56 pm

Oh, no, his pump's fallen off. Hope his shorts don't deflate.

2.57 pm

Okay, he's gone now and Babette's calmed down. And all I can say is that the whole business was entirely and grossly embarrassing. I wish I wasn't related to Babette. I tell you, I'd rather call her Godlike Deity than refer to her as my stepmother.

2.59 pm

Well the best thing about Babette's typically humiliating performance is that it's made us all realise things could be much much worse. That's actually the really good thing about Babette. She makes you glad you're not her.

Anyway, I'm ready to go and look at the van damage. I'm prepared for the worst. This isn't hard to do, cause preparing for the worst is a simple trick I taught myself just before I was born.

I'm hoping it's really bad. Then I can ring Grandma and say 'Sorry Babe, can't make it. How about you postpone your death till exam time in May?'

3.02 pm

The damage is really bad.

FANTASTIC!

But because Dad has to pay for it he's preparing to convince the ute owners that their damage is a positive thing, by practising stupid comments like, 'Well considering the back of your ute is so small now, it'll sure make it easier to park.'

Everyone else is sort of excited about the damage. You know the way people are when they say, 'Oh that's terrible, I can't bear to watch' and then move in closer for a really good look.

3.03 pm

Kate's awake now. She's really enthusiastic about the car accident. She's probably used to looking at absolute disasters, after being born with a face like hers.

3.05 pm

I'm pretending to be a tree.

All my family (note I use that term loosely)

are standing in the middle of the road yelling and screaming and waving their arms like you're supposed to after an accident.

3.07 pm

Now they've stopped cause they're getting really tired. The ute owners have each been thrown thirty metres from their ute and have to walk all the way back. So now Mum and Dad and Babette and the Pip and wart head and snot bum are taking it in turns one by one, to do the yelling and screaming and waving their arms. And they're actually getting quite good at it.

3.09 pm

Mum's unscrewing her thermos. She obviously thinks that after such a long walk they'll desperately need a cuppa. She's too tight to give us all our own tea bags, so she's sharing one between two people. Tea bags are actually the only thing my family recycles ... tea bags and this one old joke that Dad tells.

3.18 pm

I think we're all preparing ourselves for a confrontation, each of us in our own special way. The Pip's tucking his shirt in, Elizabeth's slicking her hair with a comb (that she actually *let* Mum spit on), Kate's pulling a face that I'm thinking of patenting as a cheap form of torture, and I've taken my coat off and put it on backwards, ready to pull the hood over my face if absolute worse comes to paralysingly embarrassing worst.

And Dad's getting ready to run for his life. He's just like some wild two legged animal.

Yep just like a duck.

I wasn't expecting him to do this. Of course I should have. I mean were talking about a man who hates confrontation of any sort. Once at *The Accountants' Club*, a man tried to pick some sort of wussy fight with Dad. So he acted really, really tough and said 'Okay mate, step outside' , and then as soon as the man did step outside, Dad shut the door behind him.

Anyway, I'm not looking at Dad, just out of habit, but I can hear his thongs clicking closer. Clicking is another nervous habit he's got. He jiggles, he clicks, and his pulse races when he's tense. This is apparently very dangerous for his heart, so I try to keep him as tense as possible (at all times).

3.19 pm

I'm trying to look on the bright side of this, but I've got about as much to look forward to as a clean hanky.

3.20 pm

Now everyone's ready for confrontation. Except Dad. He's turning round with a click of his thongs and whispering something. But he's whispering it so softly and with such exaggerated mouth movements that none of us knows what he's talking about. (Still considering the rubbish Dad usually blabs, I don't think any of us feels we're missing out.)

3.21 pm

My 'family' is continuing in a row towards the victims. They're singing *We shall not be moved.* I'm standing next to the Hi Ace now, trying to look like a hub cap. And Dad's running around

like a two legged lemon pointing at the ute
owners and mouthing what appears to be
either 'blop, blop devacious', or a silent triple
barrel burp.

3.25 pm

I'm giggling at Dad. And Mum isn't telling me
to shut up. It's the only time I'm allowed to
laugh at someone — when I'm laughing at Dad.

3.26 pm

Now the ute people are giggling at Dad too,
and I'm actually proud of my father. Here he is,
holding his own, entertaining a crowd, the
centre of attention, and not just because of the
usual reason, that he looks exactly like Mary
Queen of Scots.

3.27 pm

Now, Dad's holding his arms in the air like
footy goal posts and yelling 'Stop, stop, ... they're
Asians!'

Forget everything I said before about being

proud. My father is lower than a road worker's stubbies!

3.27 and a squidge

I think the best way to cope with this situation is to pretend it didn't happen.

Actually that's my basic strategy for coping with my whole life.

3.28 pm

Anyway, none of us is paying any attention to Dad, as usual, and we're all just looking at the Asians. There are three of them: a man and a woman and the sort of unattractive son that they use for the 'before' photos in Mr Universe commercials.

Mum's going up to them. She's trying hard to look like Maggie Thatcher but she looks more like Dame Edna Everage.

I'm thinking Mum must be really brave. I mean to go up and talk to these people when she's just completely destroyed what is possibly their only asset! At the very worst they could sue and charge her; at the very least call her 'tub bum'.

But then she could try to sue them for libel or defamation. Oh, no! She couldn't, because truth is a defence.

You can make a lot of money if you use the legal system the right way. I know a girl who successfully sued her parents for fraud and misrepresentation.

Anyway Mum must feel sure that the Asians are from China, because she's reciting all the Chinese she knows: 'chicken chow mein, beef in black bean sauce, prawn chips and a small fried rice.'

3.30 pm

Now the ute-driving man is pointing at himself and saying 'Ed-win' very very slowly.

And he's pointing at his wife and saying. 'Ed-win-a' like he's finding it difficult to talk.

He reminds me a bit of all of the rowers and most of the footballers at school.

3.31 pm

Now he's pointing to his Mr Puniverse son and saying slowly and clearly 'D-wayne'.

And I reckon, *Dwayne, what a stupid name! I hope his surname isn't Pipe.*

3.32 pm

So now I'm sitting on a rock, trying to look both aloof and yet in pain, which I have to tell you is not that hard because I've still got the gum leaf in my undies.

I'm watching the action.

I'm trying to visualise them all getting up and going, ... without me ...

And then I'll just sit here for a while, lose weight, grow taller, become blonde and marry INXS.

But it seems to me the others don't want to leave cause they all want to survey the damage, except racist Dad of course who's trying desperately to look like a real Australian by talking to himself about football scrums, and at the same time scratching his crotch.

3.34 pm

Well Mum's Asian advance has turned out to be about as useful as a trainer bra. So now stupid Babette has decided to lead the reccy. She must be feeling much better after her battle with the meat tray cause she's trying to communicate with a big wide toothy grin, while she's speaking slowly and loudly and waving her arms like a dysfunctional food processor.

She looks exactly like she comes from Planet Moron.

3.35 pm

Oh God no, now the Asians are acting exactly the same way! Either they've all taken far too many Junior Disprin or else they think that none of us speaks English either!

Good. (Can we go home now?)

3.36 pm

This is great. Now they're getting close to the really bad ding.

Mum's going to get busted.

So Elizabeth's trying to distract the Asians by singing our school anthem and Mum's chucking herself across the damage and saying, 'Is anyone else feeling tired?'

3.36 and a half pm

Fat Elizabeth just said yes.

Of course she said that she's tired too, because she's a creepy crawly sheep.

And now she's lying on the ute damage next to Mum. She's trying to help hide it from the owners but she's actually making the dent much worse with the pressure from her big fat bum.

3.37 pm

Now Edwina's lying on it too in a gesture of female unity. This is disgusting. She and Mum don't even *know* each other. But then if they did Edwina probably wouldn't do it.

3.37 and a bit pm

The Pip is disgusted, cause whenever he sees Mum lying down anywhere looking really stupid he thinks that she's trying to seduce him.

And Dad's getting irritated, cause he can always tell when Mum's trying to hide something. I think it first happened on the night of their honeymoon and she insisted they both wear queen size doonas to bed. And Edwin's getting annoyed too. You can tell because his ears have gone bright red and his eyebrows are touching.

Obviously the men have decided to try and scare the women into behaving more acceptably, by pulling really frightening faces.

But Dad looks exactly like he does when he's just woken up.

3.38 and a bit pm

For some reason the women have got up from the ute dent and ended their awesome moment of feminine force ...

Oh, now I see, it's because Mum's got a ladder in her stocking. My mum is not one of the great feminists of all time: she thinks sexual harassment is a pair of tight underpants.

3.39 and something pm

The Pip just saw the damage and said, 'Oh, sugar.' And Dad and Edwin just looked at it and they both said 'Bloody hell'.

Ha, the Asians must speak English after all!

3.41 pm

Of course now it seems obvious that the Asians are Australians because each of them is wearing the national costume: the blokes in singlets, shorts and thongs and Edwina in a pastel lycra tracksuit.

So now everyone is hugging each other and it's absolutely disgusting!

Edwin's hugging the Pip cause he looks like he needs it, Kate's hugging Elizabeth because no one else wants to, Mum's hugging Edwina for no reason at all, and Babette's hugging Dwayne because she's a trollop.

(Yep, everyone's hugging. Except for me and racist Dad. I'm standing alone like Princess Di, and Dad's standing in the gutter, extracting some snot with a stick.)

3.42 pm

I'm back on my rock. The damage looks pretty bad. I reckon we need two tow trucks but Mum assures us that because she put the van *in* their ute, she should be the one to drive it *out*. (Mum's got this thing about 'personally facing the consequences' of her actions, no matter how horrible, which I guess is why

Kate and Elizabeth are still around.)

Personally I don't like her chances of success. Mum's not a very skilled or talented driver. When she finally got her licence on the 43rd effort, the instructor suggested she drive in a crash helmet.

Basically Mum could get arrested pushing a shopping trolley. And these two cars look much more difficult than that. They look like those dogs who copulate and get stuck.

3.43 pm

Mum's seriously going to try and drive the Hi Ace out of their ute. I'm sitting on a tree stump trying not to laugh. She's climbing onto the front seat and starting the engine up. She must be concentrating really hard, cause she's poking her tongue out; either that or she's doing her impression of a stamp-licking machine.

Now she's kneeling cause she's going to pray.

I'm kneeling cause I'm going to vomit.

I've been laughing too much.

I can't understand why Mum still believes in a kind and benevolent God. I mean, let's look at the evidence. If there really was a compassionate God, do you honestly think that he, she or it would let my mother marry the

Pip *and* my dad?

Then again maybe God is kind and benevolent, but also has a great sense of humour.

3.44 *pm*

She's revving the engine cause she's trying to look cool. But I think if that really is what she wants she should just stop wearing sky blue eyeshadow.

3.45 *pm*

She's turning to check her reflection in the rear vision mirror. Why? I don't know. She must feel she's unsuitably cheerful for a religious person and wants to make herself a lot more depressed.

3.46 *pm*

I think Mum needs to go to the toilet. She's trying to cross her legs. You can tell when Mum needs to go to the toilet because she squishes her face up even more like a pig and purses her lips like a sparrow.

That's how she looks in all her wedding photos.

3.47 pm

Oh no! She's slipped the Hi Ace into reverse and she's rammed both cars up a tree stump!

Bravo.

3.48 pm

Now the two cars are fifty metres back down the road and stuck inside a tree. Mum's yodelling the alphabet. She sounds like a madwoman. This is absolutely normal, so she must be all right.

There is no way in the world we can drive away now.

Oh I love you, Mum.

3.49 pm

Now practically all that's left of the cars is the front two seats of their ute, a bit of the back and the last two passenger rows of our Hi Ace.

The Pip says we can sort of extricate our car if we all just think *positively*. As if. I haven't had a positive thought since 1989 when I tried to will the principal's pants to fall down.

3.51 pm

I was right.

Aaaagain.

The Hi Ace won't start.

But their car is driveable.

So they're giving us a lift to their house, where they're planning on fixing our Hi Ace, and then sending us on our way to Grandma's!

Die a thousand million deaths. I swear I would rather go bald.

P.S. Their surname *is* 'Pipe'!

3.53 pm

Now all of our van load is trying to cram into their ute. I don't think we're all going to fit. No, someone is going to have to selflessly volunteer not to go, to stay behind here all alone, and afraid, possibly to die.

I think I'll volunteer.

On the other hand we could always just set both cars on fire and then claim on the insurance. I'll do that, no worries ... of course it would mean I'd have to slink around for the rest of my life disguising my true identity, but hey what's the problem? I've been doing that for years!

3.57 pm

I'm not actually in the ute yet, cause it's my job to tie a tow rope from their bomb to ours. I'm doing it with a complicated knot I invented one day while I was trying to braid Kate's ponytail.

All the goobs are supposed to give me a yell when the ute's a happening starting thing so I can run and jump in the back with them. (I won't run of course, I'll just walk really slowly, and let my hair grow a bit more.)

3.59 pm

I'm still waiting.

Think I'll sing a round of *Row Row Row Your Boat* and do all three parts myself.

That'll really annoy everyone, so it should be quite fun.

4.02 pm

Well they're spending heaps of time on the seating arrangements, basically because no one wants to sit next to Mum, cause she's the one who got us all in this stupid situation and they don't want to catch her loser germs.

Then there's Dad who doesn't want to be near the Asian Pipes who are in the front seat, because he is still an absolute racist. Really, some people are born to show you that you're not perfect but Dad sort of shows you that compared to him you are. Anyway, it looks like he'll have to at least look at the Asians, if his nose is going to face north.

Babette says she's ashamed of my dad's behaviour. I say so what's new? But anyway Babette's trying to make up for the shame by offering to sit in the front seat of the ute with Edwin, Edwina and Dwayne. I bet they wish she wasn't so thoughtful, cause she's so fat and bloated and takes up so much space. But then again, she should be good cushioning in an accident cause she's a bit like those shock absorbing air bags they put in all new cars.

Anyway, it's too crowded in the front seat now so Dwayne's moved into the back where he's playing his really awful guitar which looks like an old petrol tin attached to a toilet brush.

He's near my sisters, who are both spending their time ignoring him completely in a very look-at-me sort of way.

Meanwhile the Pip's just sitting in the corner and praying, which raises an interesting dilemma. Because he's praying to God and I'm praying to God and I bet he's praying that he gets out of here safely, while I'm praying he falls off the back, I wonder who'll win. I better stop writing just for a moment and concentrate to make sure that I do.

4.05 pm

Now they're starting up the engine.

(Guess the Pip won.) It sounds like Babette coughing in the morning, but without the slag spit into the toilet bowl.

4.06 pm

Now the engine's warming up and spluttering a lot it sounds exactly like Dad does when Babette tries to kiss him.

4.07 pm

Dad just called out, 'We're off!'
  So I yelled back, 'I know.'

4.08 pm

Typical. They've all just left without me again.

4.08 and a half pm

You know, at first I was peed off that they'd deserted me, and I felt really lost and lonely, but now I can say I'm honestly beginning to see the up side of being an orphan.

4.10 pm

And now, just when I've decided that it won't be all that bad to be able to do whatever I want for the rest of my life, they've turned around and come back to get me!

4.12 pm

Edwin just said they're not actually going to

pick me up, cause they reckon there's not enough room and I weigh too much.

Who does he think he is to be so rude to me — a member of my family, or what?

4.13 pm

Well now of course I want to get in the ute.

Just because.

I'm going to suggest either Elizabeth sits on Mum's knee, or Kate sits on the floor, or that Babette should just suck in her breath and her stomach, just a little bit, cause otherwise the whole world could implode.

4.14 pm

They're trying to make me feel better by saying they'll tow me along behind.

I'm glad they're not trying to make me feel *worse*.

4.15 pm

They said I can wear Dwayne's rollerblades while they tow me.

Wow, I didn't think Dwayne was that cool.

4.15 and one fraction of a second pm

He's not, he made them himself out of four old hair curlers and two huge elastic bands.

4.18 pm

I realise I've got no choice in all this. If I stay I die. If I go I die. But at least if I go along with them they can watch me slowly fade away and all feel really bad about it.

I've got heaps of toilet paper wrapped around my knees and elbows and I'm wearing the Tupperware biscuit container on my head, to act as a sort of helmet. It's really hard to concentrate on doing this right, especially in front of all my smart arse family who are yelling worlds of encouragement at me like, 'Don't hurt yourself!'

Gee, thanks for reminding me.

It's pretty embarrassing being towed along like this. I hope I don't get tinea from using Dickwit's hair curlers. He certainly looks like he's got a vile disease.

You know, sometimes I wonder why God invented boys. I reckon they were just a mistake. Maybe God got distracted while making the perfect world. She was probably watching television at the time.

4.22 pm

I'm still being towed.

I'm trying to type, while I roll along.

Oh, why is life so complicated? Why do we have to try so hard? Why do we have to fix this stupid Hi Ace? It's ugly and uncomfortable and it puts boys off.

I can't believe we have to go to the Pipes' house to fix the Hi Ace. Couldn't we just be weak, pathetic and sensible, give up and catch a cab home? I'll pay with my pocket money. I'll have to do it in instalments of course cause I don't get very much, but hey I can handle paying $1.10 a week for the rest of my life, and my children's lives and their children's too. Yep, I'll pay for the cab. I'll get a job, I'll work in a factory, I'll be a chicken sexer, I'll dance in my undies on *Search for a Star* ... just get me out of here!

4.23 pm

I just told Mum that I think we should catch a cab home and let the Pipes go on by themselves. And Mum said we can't possibly do that because it would be rude to just abandon the Pipes and to disappoint them after all this.

What is she talking about?

Talk about self delusion! Doesn't the woman realise that leaving these people alone and without us would be the nicest thing our family's ever done!

I'm sure that secretly our disappearance is just what they're longing for. So it would be nice for our family to fulfil someone's dream, instead of constantly fulfilling their nightmares.

4.35 pm

We're still here, rumbling along, like some mutant centipede, and to tell you the truth I'd rather be a pus-filled boil on Meatloaf's bum.

What if someone sees us? What will I do? Where's Dad's balaclava when you need it? Maybe Mum could knit *me* one ... really, really, fast! I doubt it, she's too busy knitting a bikini for Kate. I bet when she finishes, Kate'll never even touch it and creeply crawly Elizabeth will wear the bits as ear muffs.

6.09 pm

Well I've been travelling like this for a long

time and I'm bored and depressed. And what's really depressing is that I'm not enjoying my depression at all.

God this is tedious. 'Tedious': that's from the Latin word tedium, meaning tedious.

I wish I was in my Latin class now, learning a language that dead people speak, that's how bored I am.

This is hell. For a while there Edwin was driving so slowly it was easier to walk behind the ute and just carry the curlerblades. At one point I completely lost concentration, went into a dream world of my own and actually overtook the ute.

None of us even noticed for quite a long time until Edwin mistook me for a feral pig and tried to run me off the road with his bull bar.

Anyway, after that I was allowed to sit on the roof of the ute, and that's where I'm lying right now. At least the only thing I have to watch out for is low slung power lines and overhead bridges.

I guess I'm pretty safe here, although about ten minutes ago my foot accidentally dangled over the windscreen and Edwina tried to shoot it.

6.21 pm

It's getting dark now. It's hard to write. At the moment I'm lying face down on the ute roof, hiding from a bird that wants to nest on me. Actually I'm almost grateful for its attention.

If it asked me on a date I'd probably go.

9.42 pm

I think we're arriving.
It's absolutely pitch dark but I can see lots and lots of lights all in a bunch. These guys must be really loaded and live in some sort of mansion.

9.43 pm

They live in a caravan park.
I wish I was dead.

9.44 pm

My life is a toilet!

From, *fleur*

4th January
6 am

Dear Whatever-your-name-is of Paradise Island,

Well today is the day after yesterday and it's heaps worse. But then isn't life exactly like that? Just when you think that your whole existence is so bad it couldn't possibly get any worse, it does.

And just when things are so good that you think they can't get any better, they get heaps worse as well!

How's life in Paradise Island? If it's good I don't want to know.

6.05 am

I'm still alive. Unfortunately. I just told Mum my life is a toilet and she said, 'Yes, you look a little flushed'. This is actually the best joke that my mother's ever made ... except for Elizabeth and Kate.

10 am

Now it's 10. I've pretended to be asleep for the

past four hours. It was incredibly boring. I guess I did it to prove a point, but now I'm not sure what it was.

Anyway, my fake sleep has just been rudely interrupted by the sound of Dingbat Dwayne Puniverse trying to be quiet. Nothing in the galaxy is more irritating than the stupid stifled wiffle waffle sounds of someone trying not to make a noise. It goes on so long and it's much more painful than just a sudden deafening major interruption. Give me something loud, short and quickly over any day. Like those mini kaftans that I hear were big in the seventies.

(Actually if I was a bit older and not such a virgin I could have made some witty *sexual* reference here. But because I'm young I can't think of one. Basically I'm still at that stage where I take sex very seriously. I reckon this'll probably continue at least until I get the moan right. Meanwhile I just practise my tonguies on a *Lifesaver*.)

Anyway, I spent the night in Dingbat's annexe. In case you don't know, an annexe is what you call a cheap flap of canvas stuck on the end of someone's caravan, and a dingbat is the son of Edwin and Edwina.

The fact that Mum and Dad let me sleep in the same 'room' as a 'boy' proves just how ugly he really is. If he'd been good looking you can be sure they'd have made me stay in another caravan park!

He didn't sleep at all last night. He scratched and hummed and wrote some stuff. I think he felt uncomfortable having a girl lie so close, but I couldn't care less. I mean sure I may have made him feel uncomfortable, but he made *me* want to puke!

Lying next to him was exactly like sleeping next to a rotten potato.

I tell you, if he so much as looks in my direction I'm going to have him arrested. I mean I can understand that he finds me irresistible, but if he touches me, he's dead.

And if he touches himself, the way boys do, then ... I'll go and tell his mother.

I had to sleep on a stretcher bed!

Basically stretcher beds are just the right size for one leg and a head. They don't let you move at all and, come to think of it, don't let you sleep at all either. In fact, the only reason stretcher beds are even *called* this is because if you want to believe they are actually beds you have to stretch your imagination.

I missed out on a real bed because I fell unconscious with horror on the ute roof as soon as we arrived at the caravan park. So all the beds inside the Pipes' caravan were grabbed by the selfish pigs who were awake.

I really find it hard to believe that for the past fifteen years my mother's been telling me to shut up and go to sleep, and when I finally do I get punished.

Call me wild, call me crazy (call me incredibly gorgeous and divine) but I cannot believe it.

10.05 am

Anyway I told Kate to tell me what happened when we arrived last night, you know like just who slept with who and she said

'Why should I tell you?'

and I was going to say because if you don't I'll put a curse on you and weevils will eat out your eyes, but I couldn't be bothered saying all of that so I just said, 'Well because!' and she said, 'Because why?'

so I said, 'Cause if you don't I'll tell Mum.'

and she said, 'Will not!'

so I said, 'Will too!'

so she said, 'You're lying.'

so I said, 'I would never lie to you.'

which immediately shut us both up cause we knew this was a lie.

After that I told Elizabeth I'd give her five bucks if she told me all the goss. But she said I was pathetic offering her five dollars to give her own sister information. So I felt really bad till she announced all of a sudden that if I gave her seven bucks she'd speak.

Anyway in the end Edwina told me what had happened cause she's a complete and total gossip. She loves to talk so much that I made her pay me to listen!

So Edwina reckoned that while I was flaked out, all the grown ups (a description really only meaning that they've got as tall as they can and soon they'll start to shrink) spent three whole hours fighting over sleeping arrangements.

Edwin came up with the first plan and said that Dad should sleep with Babette, Mum should sleep with the Pip, and the two loser sisters should sleep in a bed together. But Elizabeth said she wouldn't sleep with Kate because Kate's stupid face makes Kate snore, and the noise makes Elizabeth want to kill her. (If I'd been awake I would have said, 'Yeh, so what, go and sleep with Kate'). So Elizabeth said she'd sleep with Mum, which made the Pip feel so thrilled that he did a little dance of joy and sang the Polish national anthem. Then Babette said that if my mum didn't have to sleep with the Pip then she wasn't going to sleep with *her* husband either. So Dad and the

Pip slept together, on deckchairs, on the patio, by the barbie, underneath the hanging plastic plants poked into plastic pots. And Babette slept on the floor upstairs right next to Kate, where she used her flabby arms as ear muffs and was more than adequately cushioned from the floor by her big fat bum and possum hairdo.

Anyway, they all slept like logs. (Whatever that means.)

Those of us who didn't sleep well last night are lying in my bed suffering.

I am alone.

10.07 am

Okay I'm still on my torture rack. I'm suffering in silence, but I'm whimpering at the same time cause there's no point in suffering in silence at all if no one's going to notice.

Now that I'm finally awake I can see from my bed that breakfast has been put away.

Good.

My mother is the worst cook in the history of the world. She can't open a can of shoe polish without making it go off. So this morning's breakfast was the emergency cocktail frankfurts from the esky that Mum always carries like a handbag on long trips.

We eat frankfurts quite a lot. They look disgusting, taste off and are really bad for you. So usually at times like this we're encouraged to put the frankfurts in chip sandwiches and add tomato sauce and cheese paste. This way we get to disguise their disgusting taste and at the same time cover the five basic food groups.

(p.s. If you don't have cocktail frankfurts on Paradise Island and don't know what they are then I am definitely NOT going to describe one for you.)

For a moment I thought tonight might be a great break from Mum's culinary plop because the Pipes've invited us over to dinner.

I have a suspicion they feel sorry for us, which of course comes as no surprise because the whole world should. In fact I reckon everyone who knows us feels sorry for us, and has done since ages before the accident.

Anyway, the Pipes run a Chinese restaurant in a huge double caravan next door to their home, so dinner there could have been exciting. But Mum in her typical selfishness said, 'Oh dinner, that'll be nice, and I'll cook!'

I guess you should know that Mum has always been the Hitler of cooking. When I had parties as a kid, I always wrote on each invitation; 'Food, BYO'.

At school no one ever wanted to eat any of my lunch, and that included me.

Everyone else I know has a mother who cooks all the time. I wish mine did. But then again, on second thoughts, I should probably be grateful that she doesn't.

I just wish she would stop *trying* to cook. I mean if her cooking was an animal struggling for life, the vet would put it to sleep.

But the worst thing about eating with Mum and the Pip is the religious grace they make us do before meals. This is when Mum sings a little poem that she's made up, accompanied by the Pip who plays the toy ukelele he won at the church *Look Like a Slug Parade*. This morning's prayer rhymed 'caravan' with 'frying pan'.

10.10 am

Now it's about ten past ten, but hey who's counting.

Nothing's happening.

I am incredibly depressed. I haven't felt this

bad since I found out I'd spent all night at the annual school dance with the back of my dress tucked into my underpants.

10.14 am

Well, I finally got out of bed but then I heard some really bad news so now I'm back in bed again. Most people look sad when they hear bad news but I prefer to look happy, because if I just looked sad like I always do then for sure nobody would notice.

This bad news is unbelievable. To think that today was going to be the first day of the rest of my life!

Now it's going to have to be tomorrow.

I'm trying to be aloof and alone but it's a bit hard since Dwayne rolled up the annexe walls while I was out and when I came back I discovered that the concrete floor of our pathetic annexe is a public footpath during the day! So that's where I am, depressed and alone, on a stretcher in the middle of a pedestrian thoroughfare.

But I'm trying to pretend like this is completely normal, and the thing that's incredibly annoying is that everyone else seems to think it really *is*.

If only someone would say 'What's the matter?' so that I could groan and say 'Nothing'.

For once I'd like to be the centre of attention, or for twice, three times, four, forever.

When I grow up I'm going to be an actor and get all the attention I want. I played the lead dead body in last year's school play, and I would have been just perfect if I hadn't sneezed. And then sworn.

When I came off stage Mum told me my hair had looked nice. In the first place this means she couldn't find anything else to say good things about and in the second place it means that my hair probably looked like either a coconut shell or the hairdo Julie Andrews wore as a nun in *The Sound of Music*.

When Mum grows up she wants to be Julie Andrews in *The Sound of Music*.

When I grow up I'm not going to be an adult. Why would I want to turn into a complete and utter bad haircutted zombie, and to top it off pay full price at the movies?

10.20 am

Well anyway, the bad news I heard was that the caravan park's got no water and I need special permission from the park manager to flush the toilet, wash my hair and even clean my teeth. What a joke. I haven't asked permission for anything so stupid since I was five and asked to go to the toilet, was told I had to wait, burst into tears, got a cuddle from the teacher and then weed all over her lap.

Edwina the gasbag reckons the smidgin of water they do have in the caravan park is because of an elaborate but limited underground pumping system designed and built by Dwayne. Trust him to come up with something *boring* ...

So anyway, as far as teeth go I don't care. If I get holes Dad'll have to pay for them, and if my teeth go all mouldy green and smelly, it can only help to keep my family at a distance.

Of course we're all victims of the water shortage, but it's much much worse for me, because ... I'm an Aquarian.

Edwina reckons it hasn't rained here for fourteen years and all the stored water ran out in 1982 when Bertha, the thing who runs the general store, shot four holes in the water tank while she was trying to kill her husband. She missed him with the bullets but he died anyway when he dived into the tank through a gap in its lid and Bertha jumped in to save him and landed square on his head.

This sort of story about fighting husbands and wives trying to kill each other doesn't surprise me one little bit. My mum tried to kill my dad once. She bought this really sexy outfit and then she put it on.

Anyway, the tank isn't even there anymore because the family that runs Mini Golf Land up the road stole it to use as a high eighteenth hole.

So Bertha is a murderer, but she never went to prison. They decided that running a general store in a caravan park was punishment enough.

10.35 am

My hair looks like a damp Chux Superwipe.

So I've decided to tell the manager that I have to wash it because if anyone sees it all lank and greasy I will, without doubt die.

Basically I'm pleading on medical grounds.

10.39 am

Well I went to see the manager. He wasn't very hard to find because this pathetic park only has three caravans, a general store, a workshed and a Chinese restaurant, and the manager's office has got MANAGER written in huge letters on the door — you know, in case he gets lost.

His name is Wilbur and he's Aboriginal. This is pretty rough on racist Dad but worse for over sensitive Mum who told me that now none of us can use the words 'night' or 'dark', or refer to any colour browner than beige.

This probably also means Mum won't let us watch telly here, because, you guessed it, it's coloured.

10.39 and a half am

I've discovered that Wilbur is the only one in this whole stupid hole who gets clear reception on his telly. All the others have tellys in their caravans, but because they can't get pictures they just use them as expensive radios.

Edwina, the woman of the tireless tongue, reckons Wilbur's garden was the first filled with garden gnomes so apparently all the caravan park goobers used to think this might be what helped his reception. It was only after all the hoover heads stuck them in their gardens that they realised this wasn't the reason. So now there are rows of gnomes outside everyone's caravans with signs saying GOING CHEAP, APPLY WITHIN. I'd buy some except if I had little useless things stuck in my garden I'm sure I'd confuse them with Dad.

Anyway, Wilbur said 'no', hair washing was Thursday. I swear I haven't been this depressed since Aunty Joan told me I look like Mum.

10.44 am

I've decided I'm going to wash my hair. I just haven't worked out how yet. Normally I stand under the shower to think, but with no water it'd be pretty silly.

10.50 am

Okay, now I'm standing underneath the dry shower nozzle. And yes, it is pretty silly.

It reminds me of the kids we passed on the way here. They were playing under the hose like we used to when we were little, except because of the water shortage, they weren't allowed to turn the tap on.

11.21 am

Well doodlebrain whatever-your-name is, I've been here under the dry nozzle for the past twenty minutes and Mum just came to interrupt me as usual and say, 'Fleur get out of the shower'.

I don't care. I've solved my problem. I've decided to steal the water from Edwin and Edwina. I know they've got some stored underneath the caravan. It's in a can marked EMERGENCY ONLY.

All I have to do is sneak inside and if I really try to hurry, have everything ready, and go as fast as I can, I could be out in less three hours!

11.29 am

Okay I'm outside their caravan now. I'm hiding inside a bunch of small plastic shrubs, and I've stuck one on my head for better camouflage. It's not too bad sitting in here except that I seem to be attracting a large swarm of bees. I guess it's nice to know something finds me irresistible.

From here I can see Dwayne talking to Elizabeth.

I'm completely overwhelmed with jealousy

because I've got no other emotion to feel at the moment.

Basically, I'm best at being depressed.

11.37 am

The Pipes' home should be on a stamp as a real product of multicultural Australia. It's probably been in *House and Garden* or *Caravan and Cement* or something. The lawn's concrete, the plants are artificial and the fence is made from lots of old beer bottles cemented on top of each other. And their caravan is pukeville. It's had a series of disjointed extensions, like most Australian homes, including the addition of a second storey in the mock Tudor style, complete with those atmospheric shutters that are *bolted* to the side of the 'house'. They've got a fly strip hanging over the door and underneath it is a doormat that says *Bienvenue*. Then on the rear window there are three stickers that say 'I love NY', 'Made in Korea' and 'Deniliquin Daihatsu, we're hot!'

I'm going to wait outside here till the caravan's empty. I've brought along my *Golly* magazine so I won't be wasting my time.

Of course Mum says *Golly* is a waste of time and I'd be better off getting on with my life.

But hey, I wonder if Mum's ever thought that life might be a waste of time too?

11.50 am

Okay, I'm in the caravan now. I had to wait outside for ages while everybody cleared out.

Babette took forever. She just lay in there sleeping like a baby, snoring with her thumb in her mouth, and only bothered to get up and move when Dad called, 'Babette darling, where on earth are you!' and she ran off to hide.

Anyway, they're all out now. And I'm going in to wash my hair!

Ages later

I did it.

My hair's beautiful.

It's washed and clean!

No more slime-head for me!

I haven't been this aware of my capabilities and potential since I first walked in stilettoes.

I'm so proud of myself.

This is a major achievement! There aren't any mirrors in the annexe but I feel really beautiful. And the way you feel is what really counts.

That's what Graham King once told me, but I think he meant feeling up!

Anyway I'm going to seize the moment and go on a major boy hunt late this afternoon. Until then I'm just going to try and lose weight, and of course keep growing my hair.

3.41 pm

The boy hunt was a disaster. I didn't see even one. Next time I'll take Dingbat Dwayne with me, cause anything'll look good next to him.

Babette says he's probably very intelligent, which is her way of saying that she thinks he's ugly too.

3.45 pm

Now I'm out by the clothesline on the edge of the car park, looking for a clean dry towel. It's a communal clothesline that all the residents share. It can rotate and go up and down, but it just stands here, day after day, never knowing excitement, happiness or change.

At last something I can relate to.

Anyway, I need a towel because in the last minute I've had a major realisation and have decided to wrap my head in a turban. You see I realised that if my hair is suddenly clean, then everyone will know that I used their stupid water! So I've decided it's probably best to keep my hair hidden, until it's dirty again tomorrow.

I guess I should have thought of all this before but sometimes it takes a long time to see the obvious. Like the time I thought Craig Nott's nickname was 'Animal' because he was tall dark and handsome. And it wasn't till ages later that I realised it's just because he's a pig.

3.46 pm

Hey I just realised you haven't written to me yet!

Why not?

Don't you like me or what? Of course, I don't like you, because I think you're a boy, but whether you like me is what really counts. Maybe you're not interested in writing, maybe you don't like girls or maybe you've been in a dreadful accident and died. I hope so, it's really the only excuse I'll accept.

I'm desperate to hear what it's like on Paradise Island. You must be so happy: the sun, the sea, the palm trees blowing gently in the wind.

There's only one palm tree here. It's plonked in the middle of the general store roundabout and it's made of concrete.

The general store sells packets of SAOs, Coca Cola, souvenir tea towels and fishing bait, which has passed its use by date ... a bit like Mum, Dad, the Pip and Babette ... and Kate and Elizabeth just after they were born.

You can't do anything here at all. It's so incredibly hot. In fact the only thing you could do here that's fun is try to fry an egg on the Pip's head.

Edwina reckons that two weeks ago the caravan park swimming pool, which was a knee high plastic paddling pond, started to evaporate in the heat and the day after that it exploded. She reckons the explosion killed Wilbur's girlfriend, who was sitting in the pool trying to fish with the fish bait. So now there's a rubber plaque in the middle of the car park, glued to a tap that we're not allowed to use, that says 'The Paddling Pool'. I changed the 'a' to an 'i'.

3.48 pm

Boooooooooooooooooooooooooring.

3.49 pm

Derdwayne just caught me looking at him.

He probably thinks I'm in love!

Actually I was really just wanting to stare into empty space, which is probably why I was attracted to his head.

But basically I haven't been this embarrassed since I had nothing to confess at confession.

3.52 pm

There's nothing to do here.

I am completely deparrassed — that's half overwhelmingly embarrassed, and half unbelievably depressed.

3.54 pm

I've decided to kill myself and I'm going to the general store to get some cigarettes. I think about four packets should do the trick, if I inhale really deeply.

Then again if one cigarette takes five seconds off your life and I'm only the age I am, (although I seem much more mature), then I have at least 525,600 minutes left in my life and that's an awful lot of cigarettes.

Which I don't think I can afford.

3.56 pm

Well now I'm in the general store.

The general store is two caravans welded on top of each other and painted like concrete, to blend in with the palm tree. Like I said, the woman who runs it is called Bertha. Probably cause she looks like somewhere you could park a boat.

The floor of the store is made of concrete and it's completely painted dirt colour — so that you can't tell when it's dirty. But underneath the dirt paint the floor's made of concrete too, except for one corner where they ran out of concrete and just painted the dirt the colour of concrete first and then painted it dirt colour over the top.

Then they covered this patch with a fold-up card table that Bertha uses to practise her fortune telling. Apparently she really needs the practice.

Hardly anyone ever goes to her for a reading because she's always wrong, she's too depressing and they're all still angry with her about the water tank.

Edwina tells me all about this because she can't help herself. In many ways she reminds me of the magazines I like to read, because Edwina doesn't seem to care about the truth of her facts either. Anyway, she reckons the only one who ever goes to her for a reading is Mary McGillibilly and she only goes because Bertha owes her $2300 for six fruit cakes she bought in 1953 and has to pay off in kind.

(The original cost was only two pounds six, but Edwina says Mary's brother-in-law used to be a bank manager so Mary charges Bertha bank interest.)

Mary's Scottish and has either a really heavy accent or a dreadful speech impediment. And Bertha comes from Russia and barely speaks English at all. Edwina, who has no trouble talking, says that Bertha and Mary go on at each other for hours and they always end up fighting.

Every time she visits, Bertha tells Mary she's going to die in a terrible flood and Mary says, 'Oh drip dord Bertha'.

Actually Mary's in charge of fixing our Hi Ace. You can tell she knows absolutely nothing about mechanics but she's very enthusiastic. I should tell her enthusiasm is not enough, which is a hard lesson I learnt a long time ago while I was willing my breasts to grow.

5.35 pm

I suppose you're wondering what people do here all day? Well, trust me I'm wondering the same thing.

They all reckon they live here because the lifestyle is so good. But I reckon what did they do in their previous lives: live as cockroaches in some disgusting sewer, or work in the public service or what?

In the morning until 11 they all seem to sit on the eastern verandah of the general store and just look at the tap.

Then they move into the Chinese restaurant for a lunch of fried eggs, chips and tomato sauce.

Then for three hours they all go home to do their own thing. But because they're all completely weird when they go off to do things 'alone' they nearly all do it together.

All except for Mary. Mary goes off to vacuum her dustless, spotless caravan obsessively and to make fruit cakes which she sticks on her concrete front lawn to bake. She cooks one cake every single day, and then gives them to people who don't really want them.

It's really pretty stupid. Why doesn't she send her cakes to some starving war zone, where they could use them as cannon balls?

I see that Bertha uses one of Mary's cakes as a doorstop in the general store. She's used twenty of them as stepping stones to the communal loo, and she has the rest as an organic rockery.

The Pipes have about ten cakes in their restaurant which they added four wooden legs to and turned into stools. And Wilbur just has one cake, next to his front door, which he uses as one of those things that you scrape the mud and pooh off your boots with.

Anyway while Mary cooks, all the others, The Pipes, Bertha, Wilbur and Dwayne, hang out in the restaurant after lunch to rehearse their 'band'. This week the band's called *The Caravan Connection*, last week it was *Mona Loud and the Maulers*. They have to change the name after every public performance, because otherwise no one would ever come to the next one. Dwayne reckons they specialise in atunal pop jazz, which really means that not one single song has a recognisable rhythm but all of them have a chorus using the words 'I love you, baby'.

But not necessarily in that order.

All the 'songs', for lack of a better word, are written by Dwayne, Edwin bangs the piano, Edwina sort of gropes the violin, Wilbur blows the didgeridoo and Bertha groans enthusiastically while she bangs two potatoes together.

After this they all regroup at four o'clock on the western verandah where they sit in their cozzies and talk about the heat.

I have to tell you these people spend their lives in their swimmers. They say they find it cool and comfortable. I say I find it disgusting. With their fat bums, floppy boobs and saggy baggy bellies they look like a sausage machine that's exploded.

They should all be arrested for indecent exposure and disturbing the peace. Besides it's impossible to talk seriously to an adult who is basically wearing his underwear. I tried to talk to Edwin, who was just wearing his Speedos, and I looked him straight in the eyes and took a deep breath and talked about the bananas on special at Woolworths!

But the women are just as OFF. They're all overweight, and squeezed into their cozzies they look like rubber washing up gloves that have been filled to bursting point with water.

I spose I shouldn't be so rude about the women, not if I'm any sort of feminist. I mean they do everything you're sposed to do to try and look attractive, so I should just imagine how off they'd look if they didn't.

And men don't have to try at all. Once I said

to Uncle Rod, 'What is that disgusting thing underneath your chin?'

And he said proudly, 'It's my body.'

I mean let's face it: a woman's role model is Elle McPherson; a man's is Gerard Depardieu (a great fat French hunchback with a broken nose!)

6.27 pm

Anyway today, which shall from now on be referred to as *Doobiaw*, (the day of overwhelming boredom, irksomeness and write-offs) it was just us and them, the locals and my family. (Note I use the term 'family' here only in case my parents suddenly die and I have to claim part of their life insurance.)

Aaaaaaaaanyway, none of us did stuff together. Babette spent the day hiding from Dad and Dad spent the day pretending to look for her. After that he had a happy phone call to Grandma when she said that she's okay and promised she won't die till we get there.

I did my grande bouffe hair wash and Mum and the Pip and the two smaller slugs organised an 'outing' after breakfast. Mum and the Pip do this quite a lot because they're absolute goobers and they like to suffer. They think suffering makes them closer to heaven. I think suffering's got nothing to do with heaven, except that it makes you wish you were dead.

So Mum used an old plastic shopping bag as a backpack and filled it with all the treats she could find. Normally Mum's definition of a treat is just something that hasn't gone stale yet. But today the treats were so special I almost contemplated the outing myself, until my brain reentered my head and I realised I'd rather be crustaceous snot.

Anyway, the treats were:

left over devon sandwiches from the day before,

a fruit cake from Mary,

a packet of prunes (because the Pip is irregular)

and

waterless tea made with UHT milk (which Mum always buys cause it tastes so off when it's meant to be fresh that you can't tell when it does go off).

So they took the 'treats' and went off to look at the local tourist attractions: the site where Bertha shot her husband, the memorial paddling pool plaque, the concrete palm tree, the place where the river ran until 1963 and, the caravan park's proud claim to fame, a tyre that they reckon belonged to one of Jesus' disciples, left exactly in the place where it's supposed to have fallen off, just 16 km off the main road, in the middle of absolutely nothing, where the goobs'll probably stop to have that cup of tea.

Mum and the Pip seem to consider this trip to the tyre as some sort of pilgrimage to a shrine. I guess if you're not going to ever make it to Jerusalem, nowhere's as good as anywhere else.

They'll probably plant the thermos there.

Anyway, they set off about 1 and by 6 they still hadn't come back. Mary suggested they may have been in an accident and went on about it for quite a while dramatically expressing the urgent need for someone to rescue the four of them from the heat, the sun, the dust, the flies, delirium, dehydration and madness. (She did this with the aid of an improvised sketch where she stood up, then fell down and died.)

We all agreed the need was urgent and then sat around talking about it for a while.

Then just at that minute, about two hours after the original emergency, when we were finally drawing straws to work out who would have to go out in the heat, the sun, the dust, the flies etc and rescue the losers, what should appear in dust-covered thongs but four walking tomatoes carrying plastic bags as backpacks. They didn't say anything. They just walked to the caravan and went to their beds. And they haven't moved since.

That's why we had to eat in the Chinese restaurant tonight and have a dinner cooked by stupid Edwina who'd actually asked Mum what she should make for tea.

Unbelievable!

Talk about a blind man in a dark room looking for a black hat which isn't there.

Anyway, she served cold charcoal toast and soft boiled eggs with faces drawn on their shells.

I cracked up. Get it: *shells*? Cracked up? Never mind, it's just another depressing yoke.

I've got a million of them.

Aaaaaargh!

Hopefully the van'll be fixed and we'll be out of here by tomorrow.

I tell you it can't be soon enough. We've already spent a year here today.

From,

fleur

5th January
Too early

Dear Whoever-you-are of Paradise Island,

The mail bag leaves here today with the man who brings the fresh fruit, veges and meat. I couldn't actually care two hoots about the food, but I sure hope the delivery boy's fresh and ripe.

I'm stuffed!

Elizabeth the pain, who you'll remember was on yesterday's torture trek, was up all night talking total garbage. Everyone reckoned she probably had sunstroke but I said no, she's always like that.

I was in charge of keeping her cool and stopping her wild speeches. So I stuck a pack of frozen peas on her forehead and told her to shut up when she spoke.

Today the adventurers are all going to stay in bed smothered in Bertha's sunburn cure, which is cow's milk wiped all over their bodies and cucumber stuck on their eyes. Bertha says this cure is guaranteed to work, but I think the cucumbers would work a lot better if they were at least sliced.

10 am

Now I'm being a martyr so I'm taking photos of myself being kind. I've got some classics of me talking to the Pip and I'm not even rolling my eyes.

I've taken the towel turban off my head this morning and everyone's staring at me.

I actually feel just like Claudia Schiffer (when she was fatter and a lot poorer).

12 midday

Everyone's still staring at me and whispering behind my back. Either they think I'm an absolute celebrity of I've got some snot stuck on the end of my nose.

1.08 pm

Green!

They're saying Green!

My hair's gone green!

I saw it in the reflection of a hub cap when I was lying near the Pipes' ute pretending to be dead. I can't think what's made it happen: the shampoo, the conditioner — the water! Oh no, it must have been something else! Liquid chlorine!

Now everyone will know that I stole from the Pipes.

Oh the shame, the humiliation, the pain!

I guess my life could be much much worse, but I doubt it.

I feel like Wayne Coscroft must have felt when Lisa Fennell caught him at the swimming carnival pooncing around in her bra.

4.11 pm

I wish I had someone to talk to here. Where's Melinda Thompson when you need her?

Usually down at the mall. She's the perfect one to help me in this situation, but my parents don't let me speak to her. Not since she took our family bible and highlighted all the sexy bits with a pink fluoro pen.

5.03 pm

Dwayne's offered to lend me a big floppy cap that he's improvised out of a cushion. So I've got two choices:

1) to completely shave off my green hair
or
2) catch lice from his cap.

Actually last time I got lice I gave them to my whole family. And I'm probably not exaggerating to say it was the most generous thing I've ever done.

5.48 pm

Anyway, so now I'm wearing the cap, I haven't got lice and from the back I look exactly like Kermit the Frog pretending to be Michael with the Jackson Five.

6.15 pm

It's getting a little bit dark and I'm back on my bed of nails again. The annexe walls are down again now, so everything's more private. Actually the darkness in here reminds me of the womb, and all that cosmic stuff.

You know sometimes I think my problems would be solved if I tried a little rebirthing, but then again, once is probably more than enough.

I had to see the school counsellor once cause I was busted sticking a compass in Peter

Redlin's bum. And she said, 'Could you tell me if you've had a traumatic experience?' and I said, 'Yes, my life'.

I can hear lots of bashing and banging coming from the toolshed and I think it must be Mary. I hope she's finally started work on the car, either that or she's just trying to open her tool box.

9.23 pm

Tonight, those of us who could still move had dinner again at the Pipes' Chinese Restaurant. No one said anything at all while we ate, because the food looked like pus, and cause my father is a dork. You've heard of those people who can enter a room and make everyone feel energised, happy and thrilled. Well my dad's the complete opposite.

So no one made a noise until after the canned pineapple pavlova when Dad pulled out his hearing aid to listen to the first race at Harold Park and Edwin offered him odds of 5 to 1. Suddenly Dad squealed like a pig and the two of them hugged like long lost brothers. They danced and kissed and then they cried. It was absolutely revolting.

I mean why would you ever hug my father if

you weren't after pocket money?

I was grossed out to the limit when I suddenly found myself moved to do something I've never done before in my life. Yeah, I stood up slowly, proud and strong ... and offered to help do the washing up.

Only kidding, goosehead.

As if.

6th January
1 pm

Dear Constant Pen pal of Paradise Island who doesn't bother to write,

I just want you to know that sure I understand my letters would take a while to get to you and then you have to write a reply and that takes a while to get back to me and really not enough time has passed since I've written from here for all of that to have happened, but you still annoy me.

Why don't you write, Dickwit?

I only write to you for therapy. Other than that I have no use for you. As soon as we're out of here I'm going to stop writing and burn your name from my brain (which will be a little bit hard, because I still don't know what your name is, because you haven't written.)

But let's not go on about something which doesn't interest me at all.

The Hi Ace still isn't fixed and it's hot and the invalids still look like red peppers so this morning Bertha tried another Russian sunburn cure.

What we did was we wheeled all the tomato

people out onto the general store verandah while Bertha, Mary and I prepared the potion and then stuck travelling rugs over our heads in a cheap imitation of traditional Russian witch headgear. We looked pretty good but I asked Bertha if it was necessary to have them over our faces and she said this wasn't for magic, it was just in case the spell didn't work, and then the victims wouldn't know who'd performed it.

The potion needed rat's blood and raw fish, but we used maroon Ribena from Bertha's freezer and fish fingers from Mary's fridge. None of the sickies would even touch it except for Mum who said the whole thing smelt quite fantastic and asked if she could have the recipe.

Anyway the potion was completely unsuccessful but I think we've discovered a new fly repellant.

2 pm

I guess by now you must be thinking that life on your primitive Paradise Island is great. Well trust me, I'm thinking the same thing.

I tell you the only thing that's happened here this arvo is that Dwayne's grown a whopper bumper pimple, right there in the middle of his forehead, and when he tries to talk to you you can't look at or think about anything else. This afternoon he asked what the matter was and I said, 'Oh, don't worry about zit'.

It was pretty embarrassing, not as embarrassing as having a crater in between your eyes but pretty embarrassing anyway. Not that I care. I'm going to die of boredom soon anyway. On my gravestone it'll say 'Here lies Fleur, getting eaten by worms, at last doing something interesting with her life'.

9.28 pm

Just wondering again why you haven't written back yet. Are you gay?

Tonight there's nothing much going on so I'm going to type to you with my eyes closed.

todau awas botind as iuskal. I onl hjops thaty life idns pparadised island is mucs moire exciting adn try wos iand is ou can't thsn manuyb you sould call ek s9me tijme.

hip yo,

mum and dad being sexy

7th January
9 am

Dear Doodle squat whatsaname,

The Hi Ace is still wasted. God, I could have fixed it myself by now. I don't think Mary's trying hard enough, though she *is trying* ... in the irritating way.

Honestly you'd think I had nothing better to do with my time than wait around here being bored.

Actually, I don't have anything better to do.

Now I've depressed myself again.

Bum

Dwayne's still following me round. He's been doing it for days. He acts (and is) just like a bad smell, so I spray him a lot with air freshener.

He will not go away! Mum thinks he's sweet the way he adores me. I think he should be slowly poisoned.

God knows why he's gone for me. Elizabeth reckons he must be desperate. No, Elizabeth, when I dropkick him in the guts and he starts to follow *you*, then we'll know he's desperate.

In the meantime Edwina says I should be flattered cause he's never behaved like this before.

Of course he hasn't! Who would he follow, Bertha or Mary and her hoover?

Doesn't he have homework to do or something?

Apparently he teaches himself through correspondence school. No wonder he's so pathetic. I mean if you had no rules, or teachers or uniforms to resent where would the fun be in your life?

I don't know what I'll do today. I guess I'll just walk round the whole caravan park about five hundred times. Should take about seven and a half minutes.

Actually I already know the place inside out. It's just all concrete, tin and plastic, except prissy Miss Mary's caravan which is completely lavender inside and out, from her plastic window box geraniums to her fluffy velour toilet seat hat.

I know the caravan park really well because we've been here three whole days and while everyone is doing their activities thing I just walk around and ignore them. I don't want to talk because they might answer back, but if they don't say hello I get offended.

But then again if I don't say hello it gives

them something to gossip about, so ignoring them is actually doing them a favour.

I tell you staying here's like having four mums and three dads who all call you sweetie and poppet and stuff and, all dress badly.

I've discovered that Edwin, Bertha and Mary moved here because they felt nowhere else understood them, (and they were probably right) and Edwin and Edwina moved into the caravan park because the environment was solid and healthy for dear little Dwayne, (and it also allowed them to cook badly in unhygienic circumstances and not get busted by the health inspectors.)

2.06 pm

Well Mum's spent the morning knitting table cloths for Edwin's and Edwina's restaurant, so Edwin and Edwina have spent the whole morning politely saying, 'No you really shouldn't'.

Mum thinks they're both 'ever so charming' to say this but I know they really mean it.

And Dad and Mary, the Pip, Bertha and Babette have wasted whole hours talking about their weight problems while they scoffed seven of Mary's fruit cakes.

Elizabeth's decided she wants to be a hairdresser when she grows up, so she's spent the morning practising on Kate. Mum reckons I should spend my time doing something like that ... and I look at her accusingly and tell her I would if I had hair.

Actually I finally spent the morning 'gardening' with Wilbur. This was a useless big hair wash crawl, and basically involved sweeping all the concrete front lawns, and giving the plastic plants a wipe with Mr Sheen.

When I'd finished I said, 'So Wilbur, can I have some water to wash the green out of my hair?'

And he said, 'Why on earth would you want to do that? I think the green suits your complexion.'

Yeah, thanks Dilbur.

2.07 pm

Bored. Bored, bored, bored, bored.

I ask you, how will I decide what to do with the rest of my life when I can't fill the time between lunch and afternoon tea?

2.08 pm

Okay, I've just finished doing my abridged Elle McPherson exercises and I'm feeling really slim. It's amazing what two sit-ups can do.

This afternoon I'm going to sunbake and if I try my cozzie on and don't look as hot as I want to then I'll just lie next to Bertha.

2.08 and a half pm

Oh great — the sky's filling up with clouds!

Just when I'm going to go and sunbake.

How's that for timing?

Sometimes my whole life is like that moment when you discover there's no loo paper left.

2.19 pm

Well here I am lying on a blow-up lilo out in the middle of the car park. I've covered myself in all-natural cooking oil (extra extra virgin, a bit like me) and I'm lying on Alfoil to get really burnt. I know that everyone says this'll probably give me cancer but I don't smoke, and I think I need a sin.

Besides I've got this sneaking suspicion that cancer's a malicious rumour spread by people like Mum, to stop people like me having fun.

Actually Mum made the bikini I'm wearing. She used the old curtains from the living room. And a drought stricken bone dry car park is the only place you can wear it cause if you wear it swimming, the fabric fills up with water and gets so incredibly heavy you could easily sink and die. Whenever I wear it I look like Luciano Pavarotti stuck in two deflated floral life-saving rings.

No wonder boys don't chase me at the beach.

They're afraid they'll drown.

2.25 *pm*

I'd sunbake topless except I haven't got a 'top' and so no one would even notice.

Besides what use is an all over tan if the only person likely to see it is the officer of the school mobile health clinic who's female, 84 and blind?

2.27 *pm*

I realise I probably look divine at the moment

133

but I have to say this feels like hell. The bitumen's hard, the air's humid, there are heaps of flies here, and the fly swats I've attached to my ankles and wrists don't seem to be scaring them off! What I need is a bad smell to distract the flies. Where's Dwayne when you need him?

2.28 pm

Now my sisters have come to sit next to me, and I'm so bored I've started to talk to them!

Mum made their cozzies out of an old vinyl table cloth so they look like two raw pork sausages wearing big checked nappies.

2.30 pm

Elizabeth reckons Mum looks much better today. I reckon better than *what*?

She reckons she thinks that Mum'll be cooking dinner tonight. And I reckon Elizabeth should wash her brain out with soap.

2.35 pm

Mum *is* cooking dinner for everyone tonight.

Unless of course we all die beforehand.

This is a very vague possibility, but it's only in movies that people are that lucky.

I'm not the only one dreading it. Babette's announced that she can't come cause she's suddenly got severe post-natal depression, two years after her baby was born.

But Elizabeth's planning to go. Actually she's probably immune to Mum's food. With all the sucking up that she does she probably can't digest properly anyway.

I've got no excuse not to go and besides I need some pocket money, so I really have to crawl.

4.50 pm

I tell you, just the thought of dinner's starting to make me sick! Honestly, I'm the only person I know who sees a sign that says 'home cooked meals' and immediately assumes they must be burnt.

5.19 pm

Fantastic! Edwin and Edwina have just told Mum that she can't use their kitchen to cook tonight because it's been ravaged by a terrible fire. They faked the fire using a flashing light globe and old red crepe paper, which Dwayne and I fanned using the three second-hand boogie boards that Mum bought me and my loser sisters for Christmas, as a bribe to go and visit dying Grandma AND to be nice to her too.

Good try, Mum! For boogie boards we'll go and visit, but to be nice I need a new hair dryer.

When Mum first heard about the kitchen fire she was seriously depressed. She was moping and sobbing and whimpering away, and it was hilarious. But unfortunately since then her Christian spirit's rallied forth and now she's decided to have a barbie instead. This is terrible!

I'm not sure if you know what a 'barbie' is on Paradise Island, but basically it's an Australian word that means 'Let's all stand round in a very hot circle and watch pink meat turn black'.

The barbie's scheduled to start at 7 pm, so till then I'm planning to go and stand next to Scottish Mary, and force her to work really hard on the Hi Ace by threatening to sing Kylie Minogue medleys till she finishes.

6.03 pm

Pre-dic-ta-bull!

I just asked Mary how she's going with the Hi Ace and she told me it's a 'learning experience'. This means of course that she started off thinking she knew quite a lot about car mechanics and she's since learnt that she doesn't know anything.

7 pm

Well it's 7 o'clock and the barbie's starting. And there goes my appetite.

Mum's glowing proudly over there by the barbie, where she's grilling canned frankfurts, canned ham, and fish (squeezed from a fish paste tube).

All the guests, including me, are standing in a corner as far away from the barbie as possible. We're all scared that something's going to blow up. This isn't surprising. Mum's had so many kitchen explosions at home that we were personally invited to move into the fire brigade, just to save the fire fighters time.

7.18 pm

We're all stuffing ourselves with the hors d'oeuvres that Mum's lovingly prepared by opening eight packets of chips.

And Dwayne's playing his guitar in the corner, trying to cheer everybody up.

This pathetic attempt may work for everyone else but it would take a considerable amount of money to cheer *me* up right now.

Anyway he's an idiot, the sort of person who feels obliged to always make the most of things. He's never sad, never depressed and he's always got a smile on his face. Everybody likes him because of this. But there's nothing I dislike more in the entire world than really likeable people.

He's playing one tune and singing another which sounds absolutely scuzzo. But then again, it's quite a nice distraction from the smoke machine that used to be the barbie.

7.22 pm

Now I'm sitting on the concrete, alone and melancholy. I feel a strong desire to either faint, scream or vomit. I've never felt so alone and unloved. Actually I'm thinking of taking up some obscure religion, full of selflessness and denial. That way I've got an excuse for always being so badly dressed, and also for the lack of sex in my life.

7.23 pm

Everyone's really depressed.

Except for Mum.

Edwin and Edwina are trying to cheer everyone up by telling us all about the horrors and tortures of the Chinese cultural revolution.

7.29 pm

Now the Pip's trying to cheer us up by telling us how he contemplated suicide when hair started to grow out of his ears.

And Dad's telling his joke.

7.35 pm

Now Mum's telling us all to get comfortable so we can really enjoy her cooking.

As if.

It's a contradiction in terms!

7.37 pm

Oh no!
The Pip's standing to attention.
He's got his ukelele.
Please God make it snap.

7.37 and a half pm

The ukelele didn't snap.
Thanks a lot, God, you owe me one.
Actually you owe me one million.
Now Mum and he are doing a five minute grace which has the chorus:

'Hey there, God,
let's all stop
and in your honour
eat a chop'

Hey, God, make that one million and one.

7.44 pm

Great. Our plastic forks are starting to melt because the sausages we're about to eat are still on fire.

7.45 pm

I'm getting stomach cramps.

Much worse than the ones I fake when I'm trying to get out of sport.

My mouth is completely dry.

The fork's coming closer, closer to my mouth, I'm blocking my nose so I won't taste anything.

I'm biting the sausage.

I hope the world ends.

The sky is filled with a flash of lightning, a crack of thunder,

and

7.47 pm

it's
starting
to
rain!

8.09 pm

Mum was right.
There is a god after all!

I feel stupidly happy and optimistic at the same time. Hope I don't smile too much. I mean, that's the best thing about being depressed, you don't have to worry about getting laugh lines.

Lots of Lurv,

fleur 88

It's the only humane answer

8th January
8.42 am

Dear da whatsya name,

Paradise Island must be beautiful today.

Here the rain's thick and depressing, a bit like Kate and Elizabeth.

Of course everyone's absolutely ecstatic and getting right into the weather.

All except me. I'm standing alone in a puddle by a tree hoping to be struck by lightning.

Anyway the wally brigade's sitting in the wet under huge beach umbrellas that Mum got for free once when she bought twenty pairs of slippers.

They're dressed in their swimming cozzies. Mum's got a raincoat over hers and Dad's taken the added precaution of wearing polka dot gum boots on his feet. Sponge bod Elizabeth painted the dots on this morning. She says she was inspired by the rain, but I suspect she was inspired by Dwayne's face.

Obviously the people who kept their Mum-knitted mozzie nets on have had a really good night's sleep. They're getting stuck right into the bingo which the Pip is calling from the front seat of the Pipes' ute.

All the goob gang are as happy as Aunt Vera. Only difference is she's on medication ...

2.38 pm

I've just noticed I'm beginning to feel pretty good myself, but don't worry: it'll pass.

7.06 pm

I'm in the annexe now, and so is Dwayne. I'm trying to change out of my wet clothes without actually taking them off. I don't want him to see one single part of my body, so I've turned the lights out. He's shiffling and shuffling around in the blackness so I've just told him to stop. I said, 'You'll go blind if you keep that up, you know, trying to see in the dark'.

This arvo we played water polo in the puddles and tonight we're going to play volleyball, even though I know it'll be hard to jump very high wearing Mum's new knitted galoshes.

After that I wanted to go watch tv at Wilbur's. But Mum said over her dead body. And I said 'That can be arranged.'

So now I'm not allowed to watch it for the rest of my life.

9th January
day 2 of the rain
midnight

Dear No Name of Paradise Island,

Still no news on the Hi Ace repairs.

How can this be taking so long?

Is Mary missing some vital mechanical instrument? Like a brain, for example ...

And it's still raining! This is nearly starting to get deadly dull again.

Amazing, when the rain first came we were so happy. Now all I can say is we're not.

Basically I don't think I've been this bored since Warren Padget kissed me at the formal and stuck his tongue in my ear.

Anyway, today we spent the whole day playing water bowls. Water bowls is just like lawn bowls except you can't see the balls because they're under water.

That's why one game took all day.

I didn't play because I was sulking.

Mum whispered to everyone that I had PMT.

It's not embarrassing. She's said this to explain my sullen and irrational behaviour since I was about two.

By the way, my period was actually due today, but I'll whinge about that tomorrow.

10th January
day 3 of the rain
11.06 am

Dear Soon-To-Be-Ex-Friend of Paradise Island Who is Too Lazy to Write or Anything and Has Obviously Never Heard The Saying 'A friend in need is a friend indeed' and who obviously doesn't realise that you can never have too many friends because you can never get too many birthday presents, how *are* you?

My period hasn't arrived. Good. I can keep on being as moody as I want and still have a really good excuse. Periods are great.

If only you could get away with just talking about them and never actually having to have them. I can't wait till I'm seventy, cause Melinda Simpson reckons they go away then. They go away when you turn seventy, if you spend too much time standing on your head, and if you ride a black stallion.

I hate getting my period.

But then maybe I've just got the wrong attitude. I think I must have. All those girls on tampon commercials seem to really enjoy having theirs. They run and play tennis and go surfing and all that. They never just bloat out and get zits.

It's still raining. It's been three days now and there's a puddle on the awning floor. Dwayne's trying to suck it out with a lilo pump. (I suspect the same thing happened to his personality.)

4.48 pm

The pump thing worked. Not 100% but still a whole lot better than the hair dryer I tried, which just gave the awning ropes split ends.

I spent this afternoon inside the Chinese restaurant teaching Kate *The Dance of the Ugly Duckling*. I told her she could play the lead because she was a natural.

Dwayne did the accompaniment using fart cushions as drums, which actually sounded sort of okay, so long as he didn't hit them too hard.

9.41 pm

I'm standing in the rain getting sopping wet.

I'm trying to dissolve.

I hope this rain doesn't ruin my life ... but then again how would I tell?

9.42 pm

Dinner tonight was boiled rice and brussels sprouts, with stale SAOs bought from Bertha's.

Creepy Elizabeth said the dinner was divine. I said we should use it to fill the leaks in the tarpaulin.

Elizabeth's such a leech. At the moment, because of the rain she's helping Mum with her knitting. And they treat it like a religious experience. You know, like Mum's knitting is the most extraordinary thing in the history of the universe, the answer to the meaning of life, the big black hole and eternity. I mean move over, Einstein, cause Mum's knitted some bed socks!

They've been doing it for days. They ran out of wool so then they unravelled all our old jumpers so Mum could knit them again. And then when she'd done this so much that the wool wore out, they started cutting plastic bags into strips and knitting *them* up instead. If you go into Bertha's general store you can see them on sale in the corner as the 'all new, jumper cum raincoat'.

So far no one's bought a single one but everyone's been encouraging. You know the way people are enthusiastic when they think something's stupid but they don't want to make you feel bad, so they go over the top with enthusiasm and superlatives till you're finally convinced that you really are incredible and then completely waste the rest of your life continuing to do the same stupid thing ...

Well anyway now of course Mum thinks we all reckon they're fantastic and she's talking about expanding into knitted raincoats, trousers and hats.

So long as she doesn't put the family name, 'Trotter', inside I couldn't care less. Although if she did put the family name 'Trotter' inside I'd deny any association. As it is I hardly ever use our real family name. I prefer to use Onassis.

I actually tried to change my name to Fellini by deed poll when I was seven, but the census people said I was too young to make such a big decision.

This was absolutely ridiculous. I decided on adoption when I was seven days old!

So anyway, now I just write my surname Trotter but pronounce it with a French accent.

Of course this still doesn't solve the problem of being seen out in public with my family. But I tell people I do really well paid work for the local home for the mentally deranged, and occasionally as part of my job I have to take the inmates shopping and stuff.

And if anyone ever says that they've seen

where I live I tell them I found the room advertised in the classifieds and I just rent it from these nerds. Actually my parents are so tight I'm surprised they don't ask me to pay rent.

au revoir,

fleur

11th January
day 4 of the rain
7 am

Deer Doob,

Typical. Sucko Elizabeth spent all night writing out brand tags that say *Made with love by Mum Trotter*. What an absolute des-per-ate. What will she do next — put the brand tags on the outside so that everyone can see? Why doesn't she just tattoo 'I'm a slime bag' on her forehead?

8.15 pm

Elizabeth did it! She put her crawly message on the *outside!* She spent the day printing us t-shirts that say *Made with love by Mum Trotter*. God, doesn't she have anything better to do with her life — like *die*?

She's wearing her shirt everywhere she goes and making us all want to puke.

Actually I'm exaggerating a bit about the shirt, because even if she wasn't wearing it round, she'd still make us all want to puke.

Why does she do things like this? Why does she crawl so much? Is it a specific chemical deficiency ... or just a charisma deficiency in general?

8.25 pm

You know, it's really weird being here in this caravan park. It feels like I'm in some sort of time warp. Not that I've got a clue what that feels like, but 'warp' seems like an appropriate word.

Yep, I feel 'warped'. But then I always have. It's probably just something to do with growing up wearing underpants that were so big they doubled as a singlet.

I'm getting depressed again.

I feel like fluff in a navel.

Quel horreur!

10 pm

I'm lying in bed.

Dwayne's still awake.

I think he wants to have sex with me.

I've told him there is no way in the world but if he wants to go trampolining together, I would consider it. I didn't suggest this cause it's like sex: you know, two bodies bouncing up

and down. I suggested it *instead* of sex because
Golly reckons it uses more calories.

Puke,

fleur ❀

Dwayne's pimple

12th January
day 5 of the rain
10 am

Dear Soon-to-be-Ex-Pen Friend from Paradise Island unless you write back very soon,

It's still raining. It's been five solid days. Or five liquid days, to be precise.

Everyone else here is starting to go mad with boredom, but years and years of training have prepared me well for this.

Mum's started to drink excessively, but because she's a Catholic with a capital 'C' she's only into water. Her fluid retention is enormous. At the moment her body's holding so much water that if she sits on a pointy object and pops, the whole caravan park will float away.

11.03 am

Actually, the whole park *is* starting to float away. It's all very Steven Spielberg on a minuscule budget ...

It's really weird to think that outside of here nobody cares.

And inside of here no one seems to care

either. I mean they're bored, but they're not panicking. Maybe they figure they've got nowhere else to go? Well I have, but they're not invited.

Pretty soon the caravans will be flooded out too, no matter how fast Dwayne works with the lilo pump.

I just hope that the Hi Ace is fixed soon, while we can still use the roads. If it isn't I guess I'll spend some time thinking about the meaning of life, and then balance all that intellectual good work by having a quick scan of *Golly*.

I'd better go now. Mum's cooked another disgusting meal and I've got to go and mope over it for a while.

3.30 pm

By the way I still haven't had my period. I'm actually starting to get worried. I mean before I thought it was hilarious ... But now, I don't know. I guess I'm suddenly realising there are only three reasons you don't get your period
1. you're too old
2. you're pregnant
3. you have a terminal disease.

Well it's not the first because I'm only fifteen,

even though I look much older, and it's not the second because the closest I've ever come to getting pregnant was swallowing some watermelon seeds. So I guess I may as well face the fact that I am probably dying.

So.

3.31 pm

Actually it puts a whole new perspective on life now that I know that I'm going to die.

3.38 pm

I'm actually starting to enjoy myself. Only problem is I don't know what to tell my mother. See I'm not sure what will make her more upset: the news that I might be pregnant or that I think I'm dying.

4 pm

Now I'm on this lilo, floating around the floor of the workshed where Mary's parked our Hi Ace. I've sort of put the fact that I'm dying on the back burner for a while. I'm here to watch Mary at work, but Mary the fruit cake's gone off to bake a fruit cake so Dad's snuck in to work on his van. Actually I'm glad I'm watching Dad instead, not because I find him particularly interesting, but because it's always funny to watch him pretend to do something he knows nothing about.

This includes almost everything.

At the moment he reckons he's going to work on the engine. But I know Mary took it out to pull apart at least three days ago. I'm not going to tell Dad because I like watching him search for it in the boot with a torch and twenty pocket magnets joined together by sticky tape.

So far the only thing he's found with this garbage was Kate's braces, which were stuck to her teeth at the time.

He is soooooooooooooooooo embarrassing.

Dad never knows what he's doing. And when it comes to anything vaguely mechanical he is an absolute joke. He'd probably whisk an egg by holding the egg whisk deep in the bowl and then running round it in circles.

But I guess now his absence of mind could be blamed on too many worries, instead of the usual reason which is the complete absence of a mind.

Actually I think Dad's worried about Grandma dying. He hasn't had a gab with her for ages. I mean he was able to ring her for the first few days, but now there's a spikey catfish swimming in the phone booth and everyone's too scared to use it.

Yesterday I caught him trying to con Wilbur's dog into taking a message to Grandma. He was trying to bribe it with a map and a bone but Wilbur's dog is a vegetarian and agoraphobic as well. He was originally bought as a sheep dog, but now he's only useful if the sheep are in the house.

He's embarrassing, my father.

I wish he was someone else's.

10.35 pm

Dwayne just saw my boobs!

I was getting changed pretending I was Madonna, with two party hats left over from Mum's barbie stuck over my chest like a bra, and then I spun around and whipped them off and who should be standing in the doorway but Dingbat, who held his mouth absolutely wide open and then started to clap.

Help!

See, nothing

MY CLEAVAGE

13th January
day 6 of the rain
11 am

Dear Doob a name,

I've spent the morning being followed round the caravan park by Dwayne, who's behaving like a dog. It's really completely and utterly boring but I keep walking to see how far he'll go.

11.05 am

Little bit bored now.

I just told him that he's got no pride in our space, this isn't a hotel and I'm not his maid. I went on and on, and now I know why my mother says all that sort of stuff, because it's REALLY FUN. I told him that our annexe is a waterlogged disgrace and then I had a zizz wearing a snorkel and goggles. I did this to stress the point that I'm severely uncomfortable and that he should really do something about it. But then I woke up and took the snorkel out and now I can't close my mouth.

Bertha saw me in the car park with my

mouth wide open, assumed I had nasal congestion and forced me to breathe into a paper bag for more than thirty five minutes. If my mum had suggested this I would have ignored it, but Bertha reminds me of our local priest so I'm really scared of her and do whatever she says. Anyway, when I finally told her, 'It's because I wore a snorkel to sleep', she gave me three aspirins, took my pulse and made me lie in the hammock with a tomato on my forehead and a Cheezel stuck on each toe.

And besides, it's still raining.

6 pm

It's
    still
        raining!

9 pm

Still
    raining!

11.48 pm

It's
    still
        raining!

Life sucks, *fleur*

14th January
day 7 of the rain
6 am

Dear who-cares-any-name'll-do,

Dwayne and I haven't spoken for ages. I think we're both too embarrassed. We probably should talk about how we're not talking but we can't, because we're not talking.

6 pm

The water's getting higher.

Today it looked like it might start to come up over the wheels and into the caravans so the Pip said we should pump the tyres up to maximum height and try to raise the caravans above the water. At first we ignored him just out of habit, but then when Dad found a yabby in his polka dot gumboot he decided it was time to take action. So we pumped up Wilbur's caravan first and just when we'd finished doing the last tyre the whole caravan floated away.

I wish I was in it!

9 pm

I asked Dad why we have to stay here in the Park and he said we're waiting for the Hi Ace. Then I said, 'But really, Dad, what's this suffering worth?' And he said, '$28,000'!

What a wart head.

Don't wake your father while he is driving

15th January
day 8 of the rain
12.03 pm

Dear Dung Bung Whatsasnot,

How's Paradise Island? I couldn't care less. I think we're reaching crisis point. Living here is like *Neighbours* on drugs.

Everyone's starting to go weirder and weirder. I think it's the boredom caused by the rain, and the frustration of not being able to escape. But then again none of the residents wants to leave here anyway, so maybe they're just weird full stop.

Edwin and Edwina are obviously weird because they gave birth to Dwayne.

And Bertha's weird because she's Russian, and Mary's weird because she's Scottish, and the Pip and Babette are both weird too because they're married to my parents.

And they're all weird because they're still here. Why haven't they left? They couldn't feel some sort of sense of duty towards us! No one else ever has.

Mum reckons the residents are waiting for the rain to stop and they're just being sensible.

But if they were really sensible people they would have left here before they arrived.

2.41 pm

I'm spending the whole day playing pick a fight with my sisters, where they say anything and I just disagree.

3.50 pm

Today Dad decided to go for a drive and spent four hours in the front of the Hi Ace, going nowhere and just saying 'vroom'.

5.19 pm

I think Mum knows that something has to be done to boost morale in our 'little camp'. I reckon this sensitivity is something she learnt at her wedding when she probably had to cheer up all the depressed guests.

Anyway tonight she's organised a game of bowls in the restaurant, using the plastic oranges that were hanging from the concrete palm tree. Then after that we're playing non competitive pass the parcel, where any little prezzie you find in the parcel has to be given back. (Guess whose parents' *that* idea was!)

Then all of us are supposed to come up with

some entertainment, so for my turn I said we'll all watch tv.

Tomorrow Mary's got us all to agree to clean her house, what with I don't know. A pool filter?

And Babette's going to teach us aerobics. I guess we'll all just watch her roll around in her leotard and try to stop ourselves getting seasick. Then some time the Pip's going to teach us soccer using the huge fibreglass golfball the 'borrowed' from Mini Golf Land and wearing the uniforms Mum and Edwina have made by stapling Bertha's souvenir tea towels together.

I realise all this activity probably sounds very exciting, especially if you live on a desert island, but I can't get excited at all. I guess I'm sort of genetically deficient in that specific department.

And as well I'm too depressed. My hair isn't growing and it's still a stupid colour and there's not a zot I can do about it. Mum's knitted me a thing like a shower cap, but when I wear it I look like a tea pot. Dwayne tried dyeing my hair back to basic mouse but he turned it mauve instead. And I knew as soon as he'd finished that it was a disaster. Cause when I asked if I could have a look he said, 'I think it'd be better if you didn't.'

11.04 pm

I wish I was back in my bed now, recovering from life. Apparently for some people life's a mystery, a dream, a thrilling adventure. To me it's like having pooh on your shoe.

Anyway, where was I? Oh yes, here. I'm sitting in the restaurant trying to get someone to talk to me.

Normally I do this quite successfully by looking like I want to be alone.

I'm wearing some dry clothes that I found in Edwina's wardrobe. I'd look quite hip if this were the eighties.

The restaurant's empty.

I think I may as well leave.

11.06 pm

Dwayne's just come in. I definitely should leave.

11.07 pm

He's sitting down beside me.
Vomit. He just kissed me on the head.
Gross offness he's singing a song.

He reckons the song's called 'Fleur le beurre de mon coeur', but the way he says it with his broad Australian accent it translates to mean either 'Fleur the butter of my heart' or 'Fleur the bur of my bum'.

Puke, puke, puke! Looks like he definitely loves me!

Why do I always attract the losers? Where are the truly great guys? I want someone rich who's really mature ... and preferably about to die.

Anyway, he's singing the song wearing a dinner suit that I bet he's borrowed from Bertha. I know she's been thinking of passing it on to her son, but seeing she doesn't have one, she must've decided to lend it to Dwayne.

The suit stinks just like a pine forest. There's that air freshener again. He probably sprayed it to make all the wardrobe stinks go away. So now he doesn't stink like a wardrobe at all, he stinks like a public loo in the alps.

I could never do something like that, cause canned pine forests give me asthma.

Sometimes I wonder why I get asthma. When I was a kid I used to get really embarrassed about it. Then I went through a stage where I was actually quite proud, because I realised that many highly creative people throughout history have had a similar sort of chronic illness. I like this theory because it's romantic and besides, considering I don't have a creative bone in my body, I think it's nice that I have creative lungs.

Actually I wouldn't be surprised if my asthma is my parents' fault because as a kid I always got it whenever they fought. Mind you I also get it watching the rude bits in movies, so there's probably no correlation.

Once a specialist tried to find the cause and asked about my family medical history, but all I know is that Dad gets flatulence and Mum burps into hankies and I don't think these have given me asthma. Although I must say that just thinking about it has made it hard to breathe.

11.15 pm

Anyway, I'm starting to cry. Not for any reason at all, except that it seems quite poetic in a Meryl Streep sort of way.

11.15 and a half pm

I'm wondering what Dwayne will do, how will he cope, will he hug me and hold me and speak of his love?

11.16 pm

No, he's holding me nervously in his fingertips and saying, 'Cheer up, don't cry. You're not alone. The decor here depresses me too.'

Holy malooly, what a jerk!

16th January
day 9 of the rain
10 am

Dear Do wa wa whatsaname,

It's still raining, the car's not fixed and I'm pretending to be a rock.

10.14 am

I walked into Bertha's general store this morning, tripped on the floor and fell under the fortune-telling card table. Two of the legs broke and the table fell on my head. Then Bertha came up and told me very loudly that this was a sign of really bad luck. You don't say! I think I've cracked my skull.

Anyway, that's where I am now: lying under the table.

10.15 am

I'm ignoring Bertha, even though she smells like a human salami.

10.16 am

Now she's lifting the table off my head and giving me the bill for all the SAOs I squashed while I was dying.

10.17 am

I've just told Bertha I can't possibly repay her so we're going to spend the whole afternoon crushing the SAOs, adding sugar and honey and beer and tomato sauce and turning them into biscuits. I've got no idea why!

Bertha reckons this is what they would've done back in her old country.

It's probably why she left.

10.18 am

Bertha's telling me a few native jokes in Russian. They're not all that hilarious.

10.19 am

Now we're singing some old Russian songs about rising up and fighting the oppressors.

I'm singing them really loudly because I suspect they're about my parents.

10.26 am

We've finally stopped singing. She's holding me in her arms and saying, 'You are really very very beautiful'.

I just said 'Pardon?' so she'd say it again.

10.27 am

Now she's touching my hand, lifting my chin and saying 'Don't vaste yur lif moy darlink'.

Now I've burst into tears.

She's burst into tears.

And I think we could sit here crying for a very long time. I wish this situation was funny but it's not funny at all. The whole thing is absolutely tragic, cause I should have got her to say I was beautiful while she was talking into a tape recorder.

Dwayne just came in wearing flippers.

10.36 am

Outside the flood waters are completely filled with murky debris and waste, a bit like Babette's head.

Write some time, I'm nearly bored again.

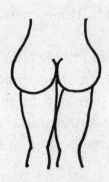
BEFORE MARRIAGE

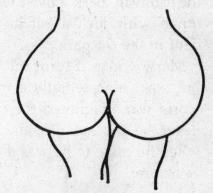
AFTER MARRIAGE

17th January
day 10 of the rain
5 am

Dear Doob head whatsaname,

Well the river's holding but the rain's still coming down so I'm sure there'll be another emergency soon. Today I thought I'd just have a quiet afternoon or else spontaneously combust.

But Dad decided to get electrocuted.

He was climbing up the palm tree to improve his hearing aid reception when he accidentally stuck his coat hanger aerial into the caravan park power box. He was struck down with such a jolt he left a three metre dent in the car park.

Mary, who as it turns out is not only Scottish but was coincidentally a nurse in the second world war, diagnosed the fact that Dad might never be the same again. But unfortunately, when he came to he was the same boring blob as before.

Ode to Dad

It was strange to be looking at losing Dad like that, after years of trying at the shopping mall.

Strange to wonder what life'd be like without him, and realising, pretty good after all!

Sometimes I wonder why we have parents. I mean they're such a handicap. And if we cause them all that pain and suffering, wouldn't they be better off dead? Or at least put out on some sort of farm like they do with old horses.

Actually I've been wondering lately if nature's set a precedent for the care of parents. I mean I know the black widow spider eats her mate after sex, so I was wondering if any animal eats its parents after birth.

I suppose I could always be the first.

6.10 pm

I've read what I just wrote and I've realised it sounds an awful lot like I don't like my parents. Basically there's a good reason for this and that's because I don't.

But I have to admit that when Dad was lying there, going all stiff and blue, I did feel a lump in my throat, but it turned out to be a bit of undigested lunch.

When Dad finally came to, Mum burst into tears. I'm not sure if this was cause she was feeling happy or sad, but she gave him a kiss anyway. It was really romantic, like the days when they were married, and she kissed him gently on the side of the face while she made a farting noise with her lips.

Then after that we all shook hands and bowed, which is sort of like our own family version of the group hug. Basically we don't like to be any less than spitting distance from each other.

9 pm

Okay, it's dark outside and I'm in bed. Dwayne's pretending to write a letter to a friend, but we all know that's impossible because he obviously hasn't got any. I'm hiding from him because straight after Dad nearly died, I nearly died too. I was walking innocently into the annexe and I caught Dwayne with his pants down. Literally.

At first I thought it was a full moon rising but then he turned round and I saw absolutely everything, which I have to say wasn't that much, and certainly absolutely nothing like the size of the illustrations in our sex education class!

You know they shouldn't exaggerate actual wobbly bit sizes for those classes, because I'm sure it only means that all of us girls will spend the rest of our lives completely disappointed.

Anyway after seeing Dwayne's wobbly bits I was feeling sort of seasick and needed to talk to someone, so I tossed a coin and chose Elizabeth. I knew that she wouldn't have one bit of advice, and all she said was, 'Well I think it's better that you find out now and get depressed, instead of after you're married.'

Gee thanks, goob head.

Guess Michelangelo's David must be in proportion.

Actually how does she know about boys' bits?

Maybe she's done it. Wow I'm actually proud of her!

9.30 pm

I think I'll go talk to Elizabeth again. I want to know who she did it with. What did he look like? What did he say? How did she manage to pull her stomach in and still breathe at the same time?

Did they use contraception? If so, what?

I mean before this revelation I wouldn't have thought she'd need contraception, because she is soooo off.

And what about sexual diseases? What precautions did they take?

I hope she didn't ask Mum for her advice. Mum thinks sexually transmitted diseases are things like kids.

9.35 pm

I'm sitting here waiting for Elizabeth to finish the washing up. I'd offer to help her but it's not her birthday, and I don't need anything, so why on earth should I?

Why did I decide I needed to talk to her? I'm having major second thoughts. I'd rather pick my nose and eat it.

9.42 pm

Elizabeth just came out and said, 'Yeah, scum bag, what do you want?'.

And I said, 'I need to borrow some deodorant.'

And she said I'd have to pay her five cents to use it.

And I reckon I'd give her anything to get out of here.

9.47 pm

I've just looked and I don't have five cents and I've already just used the deodorant!

Disaster. She'll probably call the police.

I don't know what to do.

9.49 pm

I just told her she's lost weight.

I don't think I have to give her five cents anymore.

But she reckons I have to come up with the real reason for being here.

God I if I knew the reason for being I'd be the next messiah or head prefect or something.

9.52 pm

Anyway I told Elizabeth I want to talk about sex and now she thinks I'm on drugs. This is actually a very good thing cause now I can say whatever I want and she'll just think I'm out of it.

9.54 pm

She's talking to me about the monkeys at the zoo, flowers and birds and the bees. She says she can't understand why the birds don't get stung, and I'm sneaking out the door, backwards, nodding and saying mmmmmmm.

mmmmmmmmm,
She's even more of a virgin than I am!

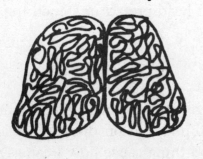

18th January
day 11 of the rain
11.12 am

Dear Duvavne or whatever,

Guess what?

It's still raining.

And in further bad news, I'm not going to die, because I got my period today.

So I'm faking these major stomach cramps. Doing this actually hurts much more than a genuine stomach cramp, but I've been faking them since I was about twelve and if I don't fake them with this period as well I'll not only lose all credibility but be forced to do P.E.

Anyway, I'm on the floor moaning and groaning, which everyone round me is pretty used to, cause I normally do this when anybody speaks. We're in the middle of an urgent meeting to discuss what we're going to do about the rain and evacuation and stuff. I suspect we'll unanimously decide that we'll wait and see.

That's the sort of go gettum people we all appear to be.

Meanwhile I would just like to let you know that Mary has been acting really weird lately. She says that she's still working on the Hi Ace but I think the rain's starting to get to her because I caught her vacuuming the *outside* of her caravan. I asked her if she was all right and she told me to go away or she'd shoot, which I guess probably should have scared me off, except it was a feather duster she threatened to shoot me with.

6.07 pm

Today I went to visit Mary cause I had this sort of feeling that she was in need of my hello. Women get these compassionate intuitions all the time, but usually I try to ignore mine. Actually I probably wouldn't have cared one bit about Mary if my life weren't in her hands. I mean I think she's behaving irresponsibly. If she wants to have some sort of nervous breakdown or complete and utter freak out, I think it would be mature of her to wait at least until she's finished fixing the Hi Ace.

That's what I'd do if I was more mature.

Anyway so I walk in, she says to go away and then bursts into tears.

And then she suddenly says that she may as well kill herself because no one loves her. I wanted to tell her not to be silly that wasn't true, but unfortunately it is. I told her if she killed herself she wouldn't go to heaven, and she said 'Do you think I'll go to heaven if I wait till my natural end?' and I said, 'No probably not ...'

I'm not sure what's the matter with her. I mean I've heard of mid-life crisis stuff but personally I would have thought she was a bit past it, unless of course she lives to 140 — in which case she's probably right on track.

Anyway, so I stared stupidly at her for an endless minute where I just had no idea what look to have on my face, and then she started to speak. She said that recently she'd seen a different side of Dwayne, and I said, 'Oh really? Me too!'

Then I talked a bit about how stupid men's bodies are, while I tried to sound really worldly, but it's hard to sound cool when you're still using the words 'pinky' and 'willy' and 'doodle'.

And she said, 'Oh I know a good body. Get a load of this!' And I thought oh no, she's going to show me the centrefold from *Playgirl* or something but instead it was a faded old wrinkly brown photo of a loser dag in army uniform.

She asked if I thought he was beautiful and I thought, wow, here's someone uglier than Dwayne, but I said 'Yes, he is beautiful' and she seemed to be happy (because after years and years of practising I'm in fact a very good liar).

And I said, 'Oh no this is absolutely terrible. Is this one of those stories that you watch when you go to the movies where a beautiful woman falls in love with a man who dies in the war and she grows old and bitter ...?' (and quite unattractive in this case as well).

And she looked at me and said, 'No, I never met him.' And I thought wow, that would make a short movie. I can see the plot line now. A beautiful young woman never meets the gorgeous man and then she dies.

She said, 'I love him'.

I said, 'Who is he?'

She said, 'He was my pen friend during the war.'

Then I said, 'But how do you know you love him if you never met?'

And she said 'A woman knows ...' (At this point she was starting to sound like a tampon advertisement.)

(p.s. if you don't know what a tampon advertisement is, then you're probably very lucky.)

She said, 'I used to write to him you know. He fought in the war. I loved him and I always will.'

And I said, 'But how do you know that you

love him?'

So she said, 'You know you're in love when you can't eat, you can't sleep and you feel sick all the time.'

And I said, 'What? Have you been feeling like that for the last fifty years? No wonder you've been such a grump.'

10.15 pm

Okay, I've put a sheet down the centre of the annexe. I didn't tell Dwayne why I had to do this and I suspect he's a bit hurt. You know the way people are when you suddenly decide to be incredibly rude to them. I have this desperate desire to tell him what's happening, like a mate, like a confidante, like a penfriend even, but considering the secret is about him I think that would be incredibleeeeee dum.

So, I'll tell you instead, whatever your name is from Paradise Island. On purpose I watched Dwayne change tonight. He was behind the curtain sheet. I could really only see the silhouette but I left the rest to my imagination which maybe got a bit carried away when I started to see him through the tight floral sheet, as a man with the body of Sylvester Stallone and the mind of Woody Allen. As opposed to what I suspect him to be, a boy with the mind of Sylvester Stallone and the body of Woody Allen.

from, *fleur* 88

Another irrelevant cartoon

Best seat in the house

19th January
day 12 of the rain
11.08 am

Dear Da whatsaname,

I don't even expect you to write anymore. I've given up, so there. I've decided to just accept life as it comes, not to struggle against it, fight or question it. Yes, I became a Buddhist last night. I believe everything that Buddha preached, except instead of believing you start off as a cockroach and end up ultimately reincarnated as a human, I've decided you start off as a miserable lowly human, and reach happiness when you ultimately become a cockroach. Dwayne must be pretty close.

I'm going to go visit depressed weird Mary again today. I don't think I can be any help but I'd just like to be near her at this time. I guess it's a bit like when you see people with tabouli on their teeth, and all you want to do is make them laugh.

2.27 pm

I'm just sitting here watching Mary work on the Hi Ace. She's raised it above the water level by supporting each wheel on a delicately balanced pile of her stupid fruit cakes.

Neither of us is saying very much, just 'Still raining outside?' 'Yeah.'

2.31 pm

I asked her how the Hi Ace was going and she said 'pretty good' and then smiled in a really weird way.

p.s. she's got a raisin stuck on her tooth.

6.07 pm

Now I'm sitting on the toilet. It's the only place I can be alone. Everyone's getting really annoyed because I've been here for ages, but hey what can they do about it? I've told them I've got diarrhoea, cause it's pretty hard for them to prove that I haven't.

Our annexe finally flooded late this arvo, so I think this is the worst day of my life. Actually I'm quite surprised. Up till now I thought nothing could beat my ninth birthday when my sisters told me they'd planned a surprise party and the surprise was that they hadn't.

All the others are still sort of dry in their caravans but tonight Dwayne and I had to move into a brand new slum. It's the cubby house in the palm tree in the car park. Of course it's not really a cubby at all, but the place that Bertha's husband built to try and hide from her (before he died of course).

So anyway seeing as Dwayne and I are moving in, Mum's decided that we have to throw a housewarming party. I really hate things like this. The last party I had was in 1984 and it was so bad that when we played hide and seek none of my friends came to find me.

But Mum reckons we have to have a party because it's the socially correct thing to do, a bit like the way she makes us always wear clean undies, in case we're in a car accident.

I'm hoping all the guests will go home early if the music's loud enough and the food's revolting. That's why I'm letting Mum cater.

She's been here at the cubby all afternoon painting the outside and trying to 'freshen it up' in the rain. This is really typical Mum sort of behaviour. I mean as if anyone really cares. But then Mum's the sort of person who'd spend the whole day cleaning the house the day before the cleaning lady arrives.

She's painting in a harness she made all by herself using one of Bertha's old suspenders and girdle, and the seat from the old kids' swing in the car park. The whole painting thing looks quite good until you paddle right around the masterpiece and realise that what looked like an innocent squiggle round the sides actually says 'Made with love by Mum Trotter'.

Stupidity must be catching!

Inside the cubby's nearly empty except for *those* stretcher beds and Mum, who's preparing her usual party food: cheese squares, Jatz, prunes and devon presented in the shape of a porcupine. It's served on a plastic ice cream container lid and a Tupperware platter she won in the church meat raffle in 1962.

Mum hangs onto every every single piece of rubbish that's ever entered her life because she says you never know when you might need it. It's pretty stupid and totally dumb, and I guess the reason why she stayed married to Dad for so long.

7.10 pm

It's about ten past seven now. Mum's ironing her fluoro party sack and Dwayne's tuning his guitar. I don't know why both of them are bothering because you can't tell the difference with either.

7.11 pm

I'm lying in bed very, very still, trying to look like I've seen something really off on the wall that's made me lose my ability to speak. It's a bit like that bath scene in *Fatal Attraction* but I'm doing it wearing shortie pyjamas.

I tell you the only thing that's stopping me going right round the bend with this whole party thing is the thought that the guests might bring us presents. That's what you're supposed to do at housewarmings, but then again in all the excitement of doing absolutely nothing it'll probably escape their minds. Sure wouldn't be a difficult escape route.

I tell you, whoever first said 'It's the thought that counts' was just too tight to go and buy a present.

Probably one of my relatives.

7.20 pm

Typical. Elizabeth's the first one to arrive. She's wearing a sack just like Mum's.

Kate's the next one to walk through the door and she's wearing a face just like a lizard.

Elizabeth's given us a housewarming gift of a sticky fly strip to hang from the door. I guess it's to remind us of her.

Actually this really is a surprise.

The only thing Elizabeth ever gave me before was a present she originally got for her 16th birthday, from the group at her church fellowship. She didn't want it so she got Kate to pay her half and then they both gave it to me together. It was really expensive clear mascara which is absolutely useless, and a late eighties thing, cause you can't see it at all when you wear it. They reckon the eighties were a 'shameless time of wanton greed and self indulgence'. Personally I wish we could have stayed there.

Anyway, Kate's given us a photo of herself which to tell you the truth is basically off. And Wilbur has arrived now and given us some ancient beads to frighten evil from the house, but I tell him we probably won't need them because we can use the photo of Kate.

Dad's given me something that he thinks is great, a 3 speed electric drill, and Babette's given us a cake that's got HAPPY HOUSE WAR written on it, because she did the writing far too big and WARMING wouldn't fit.

7.30 pm

The Pip arrived about ten minutes ago, but nobody noticed. And now he and Mum are singing a little self-composed hymn which rhymes 'house and home' with 'small garden gnome'.

Dear God, please don't let our lives be saved by rescuers right now. The embarrassment would kill me.

8.10 pm

It's getting pretty crowded in this shoe box cubby and now that Bertha's arrived with the grape juice cordial she's saved since the First World War for that 'special occasion', we're all finding it very hard to even lift the Vegemite glasses which Edwina and Edwin have collected all their lives and now dumped on us as a pressie.

Vegemite glasses. Now there's a case to defy my theory that it's not the thought it's the present that counts. I probably should be grateful. if my mother had done the same thing, she would have given all the Vegemite to us in a big plastic bag, and kept the glasses for herself.

9.20 pm

The perty is stull going in.

I'm thunking of geting out of bud soon but I don't sum to be ible to move my legs. I've had fove glasses of grape cordial and I'mo feling pretty happee. I ave a suspicion that afta watin 40 yeers the grape cordial's fermonted!

Dwayne who hass drunke seven glassssssss of cordiale is vogueing with Mum and Babette. Wilbur's playing *Waltzing Mattildar* on a didgeridooey he's made from the lllamp shade base he fund in the corner. Elizabeth is stunding on th table tryin to strip but she can't get her arms out of her mumm-mode sacke dross, and Dad is ssssssssso incredibly drink he's eating th tale of Mum's hors d'oeuvres pocupine and saying it tasties nice os well.

Babette and the Pipie have passed out on the flooooooooooor and Kate has passed out rite next to thom. Kate actuuuuuuully looks quite pretteeeee like that. She should passsssssss out more offen.

he see ya ho,

the only remaining photo of mum when she used to be beautiful

20th January
day 13 of the rain
10.23 am

Dear What not,

Mum's absolutely furious with me for getting off my face last night.

She said, 'How dare you behave like that!'

And I said, 'Well everyone else did.'

And she said, 'If everyone else jumped off the Harbour Bridge would *you*?'

And I said, 'It would depend why they were jumping.'

To tell you the truth this didn't help the situation at all because oldies just hate any argument that can't be finished with the use of a corny old cliche like 'because I said so', 'Go and ask your father' or 'Be good, Santa's watching.'

So anyway Mum's having an attack because of last night. Basically Mum finds it hard to accept that I've grown up, which is why she has never gone out and bought me a bra and just thinks I should wear tight singlets.

Anyway, Mum says I danced with Dwayne last night, and actually let him touch my arm. She says I made her feel embarrassed. Yeah well I'm thinking of amputating my arm! She said I was my father's daughter and I said well yes that's what I thought, and Mum said this was absolutely typical and blamed the whole thing on Dad. I agreed until I saw Dad and then we both blamed it on Mum. Then I blamed them both cause they got off their faces too, and they said it wasn't their fault they were out of control, which is true cause they could both get drunk on a sultana.

After that Mum gave me a lecture on sex. She told me everything she knew and it took about twenty two seconds.

fleur 🎀

Pull your sleeves down, you look like a prostitute!

21st January
day 14 of the rain
10.23 am

Mary never turned up at our party. She told me when I invited her that she'd rather die than go, and as it turned out that's what she did.

We haven't found the body yet and everybody's freaking out. They keep looking behind themselves, you know like they're going to find it sneaking out from under a caravan or something, all blue and cold, like Babette before she puts her makeup on.

Anyway, we've managed at least to piece the story together, if not Mary herself.

We reckon she didn't know that Dad had stolen the Hi Ace motor back because she took the fruit cakes from under the wheels, and then attached my stolen lilo under the middle to try to get the van to float. Then we spose the Hi Ace began to drift along with the current while Mary tried to start her up. But instead of starting, the Hi Ace probably only mumbled and started to sink, until the antenna got caught on the rotating clothesline and a sudden gust of wind whirled it around and chucked Mary right out of the Hi Ace and into the power lines overhead. The Hi Ace landed on the Pipes' ute and wrote it off, while I reckon

Mary hung off the power lines like a mauve bat until she finally fell 10 whole metres to the shallowest part of the water course, and a current created by Bertha breathing in with amazement sucked her suddenly to the murky depths, where the fast force of fluid filled her elastic bottomed tracksuit pants with so much water they made her too heavy and she sank to the bottom.

But that's not what killed her!

It's because once she got caught in the mud she tried to run to get away and she had a pen in her mouth.

And everybody knows you should never run with something sharp in your mouth.

Mum reckons she probably went straight to heaven which is nice but impractical, like God's got a forklift truck or something. I reckon Mary's probably still stuck under something and soon she'll start to smell.

10.48 pm

Dad just said he's found the suicide note, but he hasn't got his glasses on so we have to wait. Why Dad has to read it to us is an absolute mystery. Edwina says it's because he's the man of the group, but I think really Mum is.

10.51 pm

Dad just found his glasses. Now he can read the suicide note, which we're all hoping will explain everything.

10.52 pm

The note says: 2 kilos flour
                1 kilo raisins
                one bottle brandy

Wow what a fruit cake!

10.53 pm

I can't believe she killed herself. I mean I can believe it. If I were her I'd do it too. But why didn't she just jump off the cubby roof? I mean I know it's a long way up, but I would have helped her.

Why did she have to use our car? How selfish can you be? I mean it's all right for her to go to heaven, but how are we going to get out of here? She didn't even offer us a lift.

Now we have no way of escaping!

I think I'm going to be sick.

fleur

22nd January
day 15 of the rain
5.42 pm

Dear Da whatsa name who bag,

Everyone feels sorry for Mary. But I'm just insanely jealous. We had the funeral today and we all did something special. Funny how people always do that, do a major crawl to someone only when he or she's dead? I mean who cares if a dead person thinks you're all right! My family does for one simple reason: they're completely desperate for friends.

Anyway, we all put in a huge amount of effort which is really a bit ridiculous when you remember how much we hated her. Actually its really funny how popular you can be when you're dead. I should suggest it to all the members of my family.

Wilbur played a didgeridoo using Mary's vacuum cleaner pipe. Dwayne sang one of his self compositions, titled *Mary Mary Death's Not Scary*, and everyone started to cry, but only because his voice is disgusting and the guitar was out of tune.

Then I whistled *Auld Lang Syne*. Elizabeth and Kate did the *Dance of the Sad Fairy* which of course was totally irrelevant. And then, because we didn't have a body, Bertha threw a fruit cake into the grave which we all thought was very symbolic. Then Mum and the Pip sang the harmony to some religious thing which could've been all right except that no one was singing the melody.

It was hard to choose who should give the eulogy, because no one could think of anything nice to say. So I said that Dad should cause he hadn't performed yet, and besides he hadn't said anything even vaguely nice for ages.

And Dad should have been used to performing. Apparently when he was really young he worked in a male strip club ... as the comedy act.

Anyway, Dad finally gave the eulogy and burst into tears. He talked about death and life and all that stuff and then referred to Mary as his mother. So Babette gave him a thermos of scotch which he drank till he started to sing *God Save the Queen* in what sounded vaguely like Arabic.

If Dad had been hipper I would have thought he was having a drug flashback, but the only drugs my dad's ever taken are Bex and Baby Panadol.

Honestly, my life is a one bar radiator. That's broken.

23rd January
day 21 of this prison
2 pm

Dear Dooodlesquat,
How's Paradise Island? Who cares? I don't. I know I've said all this before, but now it's really true. I just said I didn't care before because I cared so much. I mean in those days, a few days ago, I was immature and needed attention as an affirmation of my existence, but now my PMT's over I couldn't care less. Go and sit on a pineapple for all I care, because now the sun's shining through the clouds I'm not even interested in boys anymore, not since there's a chance I could have a life.

Maybe now all our clothes will dry out and we can walk home without getting arrested.

We've put our wet clothes on the line and we're hanging round in garbage bags. This is not a good look. It makes us hot, damp and sticky, but it sure beats the only other waterproofing alternative, which is wrapping ourselves up in Glad Wrap.

3 pm

Well we're all still sitting here wearing garbage

bags and watching our clothes dry.

It's at times like this I remember the family motto, 'Life was meant to be boring. How else could it climax with death?'

3.27 pm

Well it *was* looking like all our clothes were going to dry but a huge wind came up and the rotary hills hoist clothesline sailed into the air and took the washing with it.

Now we're all forced to wear Mum's knitted outfits! At the moment we're just wearing the 'shorts versions' but Mum's making leg extensions which we can button on when she's finished.

4 pm

Dwayne's rebuilt the clothesline using all the old coathangers which we don't need anymore cause we haven't got any clothes. I don't think the new clothesline could have supported wet washing anyway but Dad's radio reception has improved no end.

4.10 pm

It's starting to rain again!

4.11 pm

This afternoon we're all going to visit my mother and perform Bertha's tragic dance of the dormant ball of wool, to encourage Mum to knit our clothes faster.

Blah.

Dad being excited

24th January
day 17 of the rain
11 am

Dear Insignificant Paradise Islander,

The rain's pouring down again and all the caravans are flooded. Everyone except Dwayne and I had to move into Bertha's general store because she's the only one with a secure second floor on her caravan. I don't know what we're all going to do. This is pretty severe. To think that I used to live in fear of being hit by a car on the day my eyebrows needed plucking!

lunchtimeish

I felt a huge urge to talk to Mum today so I went and sat next to her and said nothing. I sat there so long she got really annoyed and sent me off to tidy my cubby. So now I'm pretending as usual by standing outside her door and making a noise like a hoover.

12.25 pm

Now I'm back inside to talk.

I must be going through some weird hormonal change because I've never felt like talking to Mum before. I usually feel she's too stupid.

I think she was a bit worried that I might want to talk about sex, so I put her nerves at rest by saying right out there at the beginning, 'Mum, I don't think we need to talk about sex anymore. I've taught you everything I know.'

She's laughing, so I'm laughing and now I'm crawling by telling her I think her painting harness was cool. Now she's laughing and I'm laughing and she's saying, 'Well I'm a qualified engineer you know.'

And I'm saying, 'No, I didn't know that, Mum.'

And she's saying, 'Well I'll tell you more. I have a medical degree, a doctorate in science and a master's in synchronic elaboration of semiotic nucleii. But what's more important than any of this is that I used to be in the circus!'

12.26 pm

Now she's showing me photos of herself wearing her tight 'dingle dangle' costume and I reckon it's pretty hypocritical that Mum went out in public wearing next to nothing and I'm not even allowed to wear my gym shoes without socks.

12.27 pm

Now we're reading the newspaper articles that say Mum was 'the youngest and most brilliant high trapeze artist in the world'.

They said she could get into or out of any contortion, which I guess is how she still manages to knit, no matter how uncomfortable or squished she is.

Anyway, now I'm asking Mum why, if she was beautiful AND glamorous, why she married my father, who reminds me of a soggy cake of soap with a pubic hair stuck on it. And she's saying that he was her partner, and together they were the most exciting acrobatic act in history.

12.29 pm

Well I've just passed out.

12.29 and a half pm

Now I said, 'So what happened?' And Mum said that she was on the high wire practising a new step while Dad was underneath her supervising, when she fell from the rope and landed on his head, and he turned into an accountant.

I should have guessed.

fleur

-

tiny bit of undigested lunch

25th January
day 18 of the rain
7.08 pm

Dear dadadadadadadahwhatsaname

1. It's still raining.
2. Dwayne and I still aren't talking. And
3. I think I've lost weight cause my clip-on earrings aren't so tight today.

Now that Mary's dead and Bertha's fortune-telling finally came true, Bertha's become quite famous and everyone wants to see her. I can't believe the fuss they're making. It started with the goobs from Mini Golf Land who came by motor in their bath. Then they told their cousin who lives at Woolgoolga Retirement Village, so the oldie residents hired a water bus and all came up to visit. Bertha didn't have enough time to tell everyone their fortune so she hired me as her assistant. Actually this was nearly a disaster, cause I just took one look at how old the first customer was and told her she was going to die. Then the lady got really really depressed, hyperventilated and dropped dead.

So after that I became a guru and just told all the others they were going to meet the loves they've always dreamed of, make heaps of money and have great sex. And three more died of shock.

Anyway then when the Japanese heard that the retirement village had found a new Australian bus destination they hired a water bus too and sent along lots of tourists who broke their cameras taking highly posed photos of my family. After that came a daytime television show, the six o'clock news, *That's Incredible* and *Believe it or not*. But the thing which really got the crowds coming was a totally flattering nine page article in *Women's Life* magazine (which is like *Golly* but with cellulite and stretch marks).

The article had a whole series of photos but they were mostly of the backs of our heads, cause the photographer said these were our best angles.

The descriptions used were 'bizarre, outrageous, scandalous and scantily clad' ... there actually wasn't much truth in the story but I'm keeping it to show to boys anyway.

I'll write soon, goon,

fleur

26th January
day 19 of the rain
10 am

Dear Dum bum,

It's still raining.

I'm sitting on the toilet again.

I feel like the Queen.

I can't believe all these people coming to visit us. Imagine the boy potential out there!

The caravan park is so flooded with people you can hardly see the water. And since the sudden load of people here things have really changed. We're all so bright and optimistic we're like the Brady Bunch. Elizabeth's started baking Mary's cakes and then selling them as huge square fortune cookies. When you smash them open with a chisel and hammer you find little paper fortunes inside. I write these after getting ideas from the problem page inside *Golly*. My favourite so far has been, 'Beware, this month your legs may grow too hairy'.

Dad's started numerological readings. He works out a customer's numbers by a complicated system involving tax file, bank balance, age, income and rate of hair loss, then Edwin takes the number and gives the odds on that person having his or her fortune told correctly.

Edwina's running the take-away food boat, which is so full of her disgusting food we all wish someone *would* take it away. And Wilbur's doing a really good business selling the second hand gnomes to all the visitors as cheap easily maintained pets.

The Pip's set up his own church and he's delivering popular sermons every half hour on the 'impending end of the entire world and the subsequent uselessness of money'. The sermons cost five bucks a head and he's making an absolute fortune. Babette works for the Pip as the lead (and only) choir vocalist, the donation extractor, and a badly dressed altar boy.

And Mum's set up a floating shop in a dinghy selling her hand knitted plastic fashion range which she's recently extended into lingerie. Kate helps her by modelling the garments in a tree.

I don't think any of us has ever been so happy. Now *none* of us wants to leave, including me!

To think that before this experience I thought the definition of happiness was just to be ignored by David Farago.

Each of us has suddenly found a reason to get up in the morning and then not to whinge too much all day. Now we've all got a bit of money and after tomorrow night we'll be famous as well! Because tomorrow night is 'Shove the Flood', a really big celebration concert that we've planned and all of us are going to perform. It's in the tradition of Bob Geldof's Band Aid, except the funds raised are all going to us.

I've invited all the local papers and tv stations by using our visitors as a courier service and at eight o'clock we're doing a live cross to 2MGL, Mini Golf Land's own radio station. Heaps of people are expected. I tell you if this keeps going, the sky's the limit. Pretty soon we could be guests on *Celebrity Wheel of Fortune*!

That would really impress the guys. Simone Watson's mother made a complete idiot of herself on *The Supershop Show* when her trolley ran over the host, and Simone's had a date every Saturday night since. Boys like to be associated with television celebs. Boys like big boobs, blonde hair and tv stars.

In fact I heard Mum trying to impress some bloke at her knitted lingerie stall by telling him that she used to work on *Sale of the Century*. Sure, Mum. What as?

A buzzer?

Anyeeeeeeway, back to the concert. You know I always wanted to put on a public show like this in Sydney, and really the only thing that ever stopped me was the fact that someone might see it. But out here, who cares? It's not as though anyone in the boon docks can adversely affect my career or love life!

So the concert's going to be performed on the second floor verandah of Bertha's general store. The audience boats are supposed to park in front and we'll turn on a show like this dump's never seen: dancing, singing, live magic acts and a disco scene, complete with improvised strobe lighting, (if Kate can only learn to flick the switch on and off a little bit faster).

Actually I was surprised when all the goobs said they'd perform in the concert. I guess that just goes to show that in each and every one of us there's a desperate need for attention. Ha, Mum. I told you I wasn't the only one! I think this is the night we've all secretly longed for. A night of expressing our souls, fulfilling our dreams and basically being the centre of attention while wearing almost nothing.

4 pm

TYPICAL!

Just after lunch the cubby crashed out of the tree because of the pressure of water on the roof. I was up in the cubby practising my tap routine (lying down so I wouldn't get too exhausted) when suddenly there was this huge crack and the whole cubby fell right into the water. I could have drowned, but luckily I was in costume and wearing Kate's floaties under my bra.

5.03 pm

Well just after the cubby crashed, Dwayne asked me to come and sit on something for him. I told him not to be so disgusting. Then he told me it was a matter of life and death and I said, trust me, you can't be that desperate. Then he said that he could do it by himself but he'd prefer to do it with me. So I said I could do it with him too but I'd prefer to do it with somebody else.

Then he threw his arms up in the air, took a huge load of wood from the ex-cubby and made a sign with his finger which I think meant 'why don't you go and pick your nose'.

I hate it when people are rude like that, so I made the sign straight back at him.

He told me to go away so I followed him, and then I told him to go away instead. He said, 'Stop following *me*!' and I said 'You're following me' and he said 'How can I be following you when *I'm* the one walking in front?' So I ran ahead of him and then had to walk backwards just to see which way he was going.

Then I said he was selfish and egotistical.

He didn't answer and was completely silent so I said, 'Don't you speak to *me* like that.'

Then he said, 'Go away. You're really annoying.'

And I said, 'Take that back.'

Then he said, 'You'll be waiting all day to hear me say sorry.'

And I said, 'I can wait.'

And he said, 'Well while you wait, will you sit on something for me?'

And I said, 'Sure, why not!'

So now I'm sitting in the car park *in* the pouring rain on two pieces of wood that he's hammering together.

7.45 pm

I'm still sitting here. It's getting dark. It's still raining and I look like Grandma cause I've been sitting in the rain for so long my skin's starting to go all wrinkly. Of course I'm wearing complete protective gear but my knitted plastic trousers, shirt, jumper, coat underwear, mittens, socks, scarf, balaclava and gumboots just don't seem to be enough. Maybe I should give Mum a yell and ask her to knit me an umbrella.

I'm cold and wet, hungry and tired but the worst thing is Dwayne's non-stop whistling which sounds like a budgie being strangled.

I just imagined kissing his lips.

Puke, I must be going hysterical.

I guess the good thing about all this is that things can't get worse.

But then again I said the same thing when I was two and Mum chucked my dummy out. Then straight after that, Kate was born.

9.19 pm

We stopped sitting and hammering to eat Mum's dinner, baked beans on SAOs, and since then I've just been sitting on the wood, trimming my split ends and squishing my bottom cheeks together trying not to fart.

9.25 pm

Now Dwayne's starting to glue pieces of this wooden thing together. He's doing it with a special paste he's made by mashing some of Mary's cakes and blending them with Bertha's fish bait. The cakes provide the concrete adhesion and the bait makes it waterproof.

He's laying it on literally with a trowel, and the smell is absolutely disgusting.

The fumes are overwhelming and I'm finding it dif

fi

cult

t

o

11.41 pm

I'm just coming to. I had an asthma attack because of the glue. Apparently I'm allergic to fruit cake with fish bait, so now I guess I'll know never to eat it.

The attack wasn't too bad but they reckon all the tourists were really worried about me when Dwayne paddled through the crowd of boats, making a noise like an ambulance siren.

11.53 pm

I've started to receive lots of get well fan mail

from the adoring crowd, but I've made an announcement from Bertha's balcony saying that I'll only bother to answer the letters if photos and full particulars are enclosed. I'm pretending this is for security reasons, but it's truly cause I only have the time and inclination to write back to the really cute boys.

Assuming there must be at least one here somewhere!

11.57 pm

Tomorrow I'm not allowed to help Dwayne so I'm going to spend the whole day getting ready for the concert. I can't wait. I tell you, I haven't been this enthusiastic about anything since my *Golly* star guide said I might marry Mel Gibson.

While I perv out the window I can see our concert audience already starting to arrive in their boats. A week ago I would have thought they were absolute desperates but now I realise you can't tell a book by its cover, no man is an island, every cloud has a silver lining, and judge not others lest ye be judged yourself, especially if they're going to give you money.

Anyway, we have to understand that there isn't much entertainment round here, not since the local council banned dwarf throwing and alphabet burp competitions.

Tonight I'm just going to watch the water from Bertha's second floor verandah and try that new *Golly* thing where you meditate to a size 6.

See you later, alligator.

44 calibre duster

27th January
day 20 of the rain
5 am

Oh no!

Terrible, terrible, news.

At 2 this morning a plane flew over with a sign tied to the back of it that said 'sknab sti kaerb ot tuoba si revir eht eraweb'.

It took us a while to understand what it meant till we realised the sign had been hung back to front.

And suddenly all of our fans deserted! Including the invisible good looking boys!

And our dag loser gang paddled off to plug up the river leaks, using all the garden gnomes we could find, and those SAO biscuit things that Bertha and I made, which have the convenient consistency of rocks.

When we came back the caravan park was totally empty, all the guests had disappeared, and we just sat on Bertha's top step and cried. Our happiness was dead, our celebrity status had vanished and we were just the same boring badly dressed Trotters and friends (in inverted commas).

It was lonely, intimidating and very

frightening ... like watching Lisa Currie-Kenny do sit-ups.

9.31 pm

Everyone's still sitting on the steps crying, including the men, but I haven't got that many tears left, so when no one happens to be looking at me I put spit on my finger and wipe it under my eyes.

We know the river's going to break its banks and I guess we're going to go with it. We've got no car, no boat, no phone. It's a bit like *Gilligan's Island*, without the witty, humorous, good looking cast.

This is so dum it's starting to get serious. I guess now we're confronting death. This is the biggie! Everything is a blank, while we think of the time we've lost and the time we've wasted, the love we never showed each other, the things we could have done.

I only hope my life doesn't flash before my eyes, because if it does I'll probably fall asleep.

We're all talking about what we would have done differently if we'd known we were going to die so soon. The others all reckon they would've been nicer, kinder and less selfish.

I would've eaten more chocolate cake, and been rude to more people.

9.38 pm

The Pip's telling us he knew this would happen and that soon God'll save us and take us to heaven. Mum says that she agrees but I notice she's sitting on the step with everything she owns in a specially knitted waterproof suitcase. Of course I agree she's wise to be prepared but if we really are going to heaven then I don't think Mum'll have much need for her knitted tracksuits.

Actually I think Mum's having second thoughts about the Pip, and coincidentally so is Babette. For some reason Babette seems to be finding him highly desirable. Probably because he's sitting next to Dad.

I'm having second thoughts about things too. I regret abusing and using this planet. I'm ashamed of my wasteful attitude to its resources and I only wish I could have done more to help, instead of doing stupid things like trying to deposit my mother as a recyclable old bag.

I actually think I'm developing some sort of profound international conscience, because I'm thinking a lot about the end of the world.

But then I think more about my bikini line.

I guess I've learned too late that life's short and getting shorter. Life should be lived to the full and enjoyed. Life is a present, a magical joy, and life should never ever be wasted. I've learned that you get from life what you put in. I've learned that life is for the taking. Just reach out and get it. I've learned that life is not about waiting and wanting: it's about going for it all right *now*! But most importantly I guess I've learned that:

1. cleanliness is next to Godliness, and that's why you should always be allowed to spend as long as you want in the bathroom

2. if you always find the thing you've lost in the last place you look, then you should look in the last place first and

3. no boy will ever appreciate anything a girl achieves academically unless she does it in the nude.

11.45 pm

Everyone else is asleep.

I passed out with depression there for a while but now it's my turn to stand on watch for the river.

And I thought waiting for the tv news to finish was boring.

This is a stupid job. The river probably won't break its banks for hours and what am I going to do when I see it rush towards us: dance like a loop, wave my arms and scream?

Probably. I'm good at that sort of thing.

11.47 pm

Hey I can see two people disappearing in the distance. It's Babette and the Pip, walking away together on the water, just like Jesus did, except they're wearing those huge floatie duck feet that you can win at the Easter Show if you're too hopeless to win anything else.

What a pair of losers!

Good riddance.

11.48 pm

Okay, I'm standing watch. Dwayne should really be here helping me, but he's still banging away in the car park by himself. He's wearing eight layers of raincoats to protect him from the rain and he looks just like one of Arnold Schwarzenegger's legs.

I think he's selfish, pursuing some primal masculine hammering urge while we all suffer and prepare to die. I wonder if he's doing it to try to impress me, or to avoid me, or if his brain has just shrivelled up in the rain and turned into a prune.

When he comes back I'm going to tell him how angry I am by saying absolutely nothing.

I wish he was here, though, just to keep me company. If there's one thing I can say in favour of Dwayne it's that he's better than no one at all.

Well, sometimes.

I hate tonight.

But it's out of my control, so for the moment I'll just pull a face that makes me look like a melting Mickey Mouse icecream.

Of course it's not much fun having no one round to annoy with it.

I think I'll get depressed.

Letting myself get really really down really cheers me up. Depression might feel like wearing damp socks but at least it's safe and secure. Nothing can threaten it, nothing can take it away. Happiness by comparison is fragile. Happiness is a raw egg, frail and golden inside. Depression is like an egg that Mum's boiled, rock solid and resilient to nuclear war.

Sometimes I know I don't want to be happy because happiness always ends. I don't really want to be happy, cause it's just downhill from there.

But sometimes I wonder if God had wanted us to be sad, then why are we able to laugh and smile? If we die tonight then I'll ask God that. Oh, and also why he gave Babette a moustache.

So I'm scared and depressed but I'm trying to keep myself optimistic while I sit here cold and wet in the dark. I played eye spy by myself for a while but it got pretty boring because I kept guessing all the right answers.

11.52 pm

Mum just snorted in her sleep. She probably had a nightmare, that the Pip was trying to kiss her.

She doesn't know he's gone off with possum-head.

She's been wobbly about the Pip ever since she heard him ask God to rescue *him* and take all the rest of us as sacrifices.

I think he thought he was the second coming. Funny I never thought Jesus Part 2 would wear a hairpiece.

Love. I wonder if Mum thought she loved the Pip. I wonder what love actually is. I mean I love new shoes and squashing ants, but is that anything like the same love?

I never want to fall in love. It seems to hurt

too much. I mean I've loved boys since I was three, but I don't think any one's been 'the big one'. My first boyfriend was Thomas Tweed, and I loved him cause his mum made nice icecream.

I still love Thomas in a funny sort of way, because his was the first penis I ever saw. I caught him weeing in his parents' garden and I thought he had a small garden hose.

I'm a bit scared sitting here alone. There's nothing I can actually see to be scared of, it's just a scary sort of situation. It's weird how I can be scared of nothing. But then again I've been terrified of cellulite for fifteen years and I'm not due to get it till I'm thirty.

I guess I could close my eyes and pretend I'm not here, but that's not really standing on watch.

What'll I do?

I could keep myself awake by buzzing like a mozzie and hovering round Kate's face. But she looks really tired and I know she's scared, so I'll save that in case we're ever out of here.

I've tried sticking my feet into Elizabeth's bum but when she said 'Please little sister don't do that', I felt so bad, I nearly cried.

I'm being nice!

It's probably inverse PMT.

I wish I could cry now, but it's all gone. It's

just me, sitting here, scared of cellulite.

I'm just going to close my eyes for a millimoment.

Looking after all these people is a tiring, responsible job. I've never done anything like it before. Once I had to wash and wipe Mum's good china set, but that's about as close as I've got.

I think I'll close my eyes now. I won't go to sleep. I've got big ears for listening and it's about time I used them.

Hope I don't go to sleep.

Hope I'm not asleep when we die.

I think I'll need every minute I can get to try and bull my way into heaven.

11.56 pm

I've opened my eyes again, but just to write this bit.

I wish I didn't have to sit watch. I just keep telling myself to stay calm cause it'll all be over soon. This is a technique I learnt really quickly the first time Dave Simmons kissed me.

I'm just going to close my eyes for

28th January
day 21 of the rain
Some time

Dear Blablabla,

It's early morning, still dark and sopping wet. The river hasn't broken its banks yet and we haven't heard any news. I don't know what's going on.

I woke up to a sound like a helicopter arriving but just thought that it was Dad snoring.

The noise came closer.

I was frozen scared.

Everyone was asleep.

I really wanted to frighten whatever it was away so I grabbed my weapons, a pair of rusty barbecue tongs and that photo of Kate.

The noise came closer and closer but I couldn't see a thing. Actually I was a bit disappointed, because it did occur to me that we were about to be saved and I hadn't done anything brave yet. But then I guessed that if we were saved I could always just exaggerate about how great I was, the way boys do after first dates.

Anyway, I saw a light, a very small one, coming quite slowly towards me. For a sec I thought I'd gone completely bonkers because I saw two bodies dressed in floral raincoats paddling one of those hard plastic floaty arm chair things, like you find in cheap resorts in Hawaii, and I heard 'For heaven's sake, will you move your fat bum?'

And I knew it was Grandma.

And now the two of us are just sitting here in the rain whispering really loudly, cause you'll remember Grandma's deaf. We look like two drowned rats. No actually I look like a very wet yet still attractive person. Grandma looks like a rat.

I feel a strange affection for her, I don't know why. Probably cause for once in my life I feel a desire to be affectionate and everyone else in the known universe is either not here or asleep.

Anyway Grandma says she came to the caravan park to have her fortune told. She read about us in *Woman's Life* and came to discover if she's really going to die, or if she just needs a little extra blusher.

And she brought sex-pot Jack because he couldn't be trusted alone with the cows. She said nothing much had happened in Curlewis. What a surprise!

She says Daphne and Dildra have opened up a Japanese/Australian library where both of them feel completely at home wearing kimonos with their ug boots. I've told them everything that's happened so far, about the dagmobile, Dad's experience as an electric curling wand, the rising water and Mary's tragic death by pen. Grandma was pretty upset when I told her all this cause my enthusiastic hand waving made her think I was having an epileptic fit.

But Jack only seemed to care when I got to the bit about Mary. I thought he was just being his usual wormy pervy self, but then he solemnly took off his floral raincoat and showed us he had more clothes on underneath, sort of like a paranoid flasher. So he stood there, in this old soldier's uniform, sobbed, fell to his knees, kissed the air and said 'Goodbye, my Mary.'

I nearly laughed but it doesn't suit me. Then I got sort of incoherent, like I do when I'm upset, and I can't talk cry and breathe all at once. So I just went bright red and snot ran out my nose and I said ... 'and ... we ... can't ... have ... our ... concert ... anymore.'

Luckily Grandma doesn't seem to think that I've blown all this out of proportion so she's brought out her thermos, a vinyl rug and some bickies and we've done a pooh patrol and now she's taking me in her arms (which is making it hard to type while we sit here in the rain) and she's saying, 'Oh, Prunehead, you'll all have your concert.'

Oh Grandma, thank you, thank you, thank you: where have you been all my life?

Anyway, Jack just asked, 'Who's that banging?' and when I said Dwayne he said 'Wow, half his luck.'

I told you Jack was disgusting.

I may not get to write again. I'll try,

fleur

my escape vehicle

29th January
day 22 of the rain
9.14 am

Dear Whateverwhoeveryouare,

We started today with a big breakfast in front of us, but no one touched a crumb because we were all just too excited, and besides my mother cooked it.

We're going to spend the day rehearsing our acts in the top floor of Bertha's general store. Each of us has our own corner to practise in and we're pretending not to notice each other, even though the space is about as big as a port a loo.

Mum's in the middle, doing her impression of a knitting machine while she tries to finish all our costumes by tonight. The concert's planned to start as soon as it gets dark, so we're working really fast. I haven't worked this hard on anything in my life, except for a project on worms I did for Mr Bringley when I was in third grade.

12.45 pm

Lunch was cooked by Grandma. It was scones

with tinned smoked oysters and made us wish just one thing: that we'd all eaten breakfast.

During lunch Jack got those fly strips Elizabeth gave us and hung them across the ceiling as streamers to try to cheer us up. So after lunch when we all stood up, we had to spend a bit of time unsticking our heads from his decorations.

3.15 pm

Afternoon tea was made by Grandma as well. She spent absolutely hours preparing it and when she presented us all with pikelets and ham, we wished that we'd eaten lunch.

6.27 pm

It's still raining and the roof's begun to leak so Jack's entertaining himself by racing from corner to corner with my new knitted umbrella, one by one holding it over our heads.

The man is a nostril hair.

7.19 pm

Thank God.

It's nearly time for our show.

We're going to do it, fulfil our dreams, and neither Hi Ace nor highwater has stopped us!

We all join hands in a circle and sing *We Are The World* (with me as Michael Jackson, of course because I've still got Dwayne's hat on).

7.22 pm

Now we're doing a special warm-up acting exercise where you pretend you're an ice cube and just melt.

This is making me feel like a complete and utter goober. Now I know why famous actors get paid so much to perform, because it's soooo embarrassing.

I don't want to do the show anymore now. I reckon the others feel the same way.

Suddenly I think we've been slugged with the wobbly fears, insecurities and doubts that have chased us all our lives. Here we were on the edge about to jump, to be free to express ourselves, to say 'I am woman hear me roar, I'll have hairy underarms and one continuous eyebrow if I want to', and we stop.

Or are we already down there at the bottom of the cliff, too scared to climb the rope?

We're all quite dumb, that's dum with a 'b', and only my soft wheezy breath is competing for attention with the rain. For a moment I think about only breathing half as much, but no sooner have I realised this is stupid than Jack lets off a whopper bomber and we're all forced to stop breathing completely.

7.20 pm

Dad's turning round and going back to his corner. And everyone's following him! Typical: the only time Dad ever leads a crowd is when they're all being losers and giving up. Now slowly, unconsciously we're all turning and heading back to our separate rehearsal corners, ready to forget our abandon and delight.

We all look sad and empty and disappointed in ourselves, like we've failed some huge test again or something. But all we've really gone and done is stop ourselves from getting up and being stupid!

Haven't we?

Dad's saying the whole thing's a load of rubbish, Mum's mumbling a prayer, Bertha's singing some Russian song that sounds like a cough syrup commercial and Kate's calling out 'If you don't bloody do it you'll all regret it'.

And everyone claps.

7.30 pm

Now Wilbur's started on his didgeridoo and he's doing his own rendition of the national anthem which everyone tries hard to sing along with but as usual we don't know the words. So we sing 'lalala' till we get to the chorus and then yell 'Advance Australia Fair'.

7.45 pm

And now at just past sunset, if there'd been a sun, Kate's starting to flick the light switch really fast while Bertha does the memorial Scottish Mary jig which she's combined with a Russian dance of communism by juggling a fruit cake, a hammer and a sickle.

7.47 pm

Now Edwin and Edwina are doing their own encapsulation of the classic *Romeo and Juliet.*

This basically involves two people dressed in knitted jumpsuits pounding their hearts, embracing for a moment and then both falling down dead. They're performing it entirely in Chinese, so Kate has a big job on her hands crawling backwards and forwards from one side of the verandah to the other, trailing long pieces of cardboard subtitle.

This is great. Now I won't have to bother reading it for English anymore.

7.56 pm

It's my turn to sing a song I wrote when I was thirteen. It's called *Do you love me for my body or just love me for my brain?* It's basically a country style tune about a high-powered female business executive who's keen on the office coffee boy. Dwayne's finished his affair with the hammer, and he's going to accompany me on his toilet brush and petrol can, and sing 'yee ha' if I forget the words.

7.59 pm

I've finished my song, more or less now. At one time I forgot the words so badly Dwayne had to pretend to do the flamenco while I yodelled for three whole minutes.

The audience is calling for more, more — so we're going to sing exactly the same song one more time (cause it's the only one we both know) and then stand on our heads for the chorus.

8.07 pm

Elizabeth's on watch on the roof and she can't perform in the show, so Kate is representing the two of them herself, performing *The Dance of the Tennis Ball*. They practised as a partnership and it doesn't quite work as a solo, because every time Kate throws herself balletically into the air, there's no one underneath to catch her.

8.09 pm

After the first seven or eight times it's a bit hard to keep watching Kate chuck herself on the floor so we're all sort of facing her and smiling, but making our eyes look away out the window.

8.10 pm

The rain's still falling outside, harder than ever. And the wind's belching like gross pervy Jack.

The caravan's shivering with fear just like us. Kate's finished her jumping and she's bowing grandly and saying thanks very much to the wall.

8.11 pm

Kate's turning off the lights.

8.12 pm

A torchbeam's spotlighting Dad!

He's swinging from the ceiling on some pantyhose.

And now from the other corner comes Mum. They embrace, and somersault in the middle.

8.14 pm

The act is going on for a while. It's full of twists, leaps and turns and stuff. It hasn't quite reached 'death defying' I suppose, because the ceiling is only two metres off the ground, but 'awe inspiring' would be a good description, particularly the way they manage to keep smiling no matter how high their up-your-bum cozzies manage to crawl.

Wedgie supremes.

8.16 pm

They're going on and on, and with every new move we're all gasping louder. We sound like the heavy breathing you're supposed to hear when you dial 0055 and ask for Cindy.

8.16 and a half pm

Their grand finale's getting closer, with Dad tippy toeing on a fruit cake and Mum crouching on his head. Wilbur's doing the drum roll on his didgeridoo. The lights are shining brightly, a pin point to stardom, and we're all waiting with nude admiration. Now we're going to see the trick that was their trade mark until Dad turned into an accountant.

8.17 pm

Dad's throwing Mum up into the air and she's doing a double semi demi twist, bouncing off his nose and then onto his hand. Meanwhile Dad's doing a little charleston while he waits, then the two of them turn with unbelievable grace, with their hands reaching for the sky and Elizabeth comes racing in and says 'ha ugh quick ah hurry ha, the riv a has banks haveha broken!'

Bertha helps us translate this into English.

8.27 pm

Now we're all on the roof of the general store. We haven't brought anything with us up here. We just climbed out the windows in our slippery outfits and now we're just clinging to life. We are pathetic. To think my life's boiled down to this: dying in a knitted plastic pantsuit. We're watching the water come closer and faster. The grey rush is consuming the dull brown water surface below (I didn't write that bit, Mum did) it's becoming really rough and scary. (I wrote this bit instead.)

Now I know what hopeless is, and it's not a fat boy with red hair and zits. Where's

Dwayne? It's dangerous out there.

Oh no! We must have lost him!

Edwin and Edwina are crying and crying. We all are. It's like living on replay.

And now we're waiting for the blanket of death to envelop and take us away.

I've pledged all my belongings to whoever's brave enough to try to clean out my room.

I spose I should be glad. You know what they say: 'Die young, die pretty.'
I just wish I'd shaved under my arms.
I'm starting to cry again.
We all say goodbye.
Now we're saying, 'Oh don't go'.

I tell all of them it was nice knowing them, which it wasn't of course, but I think it could have been nicer than death.

Goodbye, Duvavne?

Goodbye!

Back again!

Haven't died yet. The tidal wave thing is taking a little longer than we all first thought.

I'm just staring open-mouthed into space, like a puce haired astronomer fish.

Oh no, here comes the wave.

(I'm almost relieved, cause to tell you the truth, this waiting around for the death thing to happen was starting to get a little boring.)

So here it comes, and I go, goodbye again.

Hey, what's this coming round the corner, in front of the wave?

Is it a bird, is it a plane, no it's Dwayne the crater head in a big wooden boat.

So that's what he was making!

It looks exactly like the Ark but with only one smelly animal on board.

It must be powered by the Hi Ace engine. And it's got a sail made from what looks like the floral sheet divider in our annexe. I can tell that's it cause I can see the peep holes that I cut in it.

I think the boat's made out of the old wood from our cubby cause it's got 'mum lovw eith dy mabe trettor' written round the sides.

This is fantastic.

What a great guy Dwayne is!

Pity he's so ugly.

8.45 pm

The wave's arrived, the water's amazing, but here we are SAVED.

We're saved!

We're all up on the boat but we're still yelling shoving and pushing. It's a sign that things are getting back to normal.

There's a cabin, so we're nearly dry. Mum's out steering with Dad on the watch while Bertha's navigating using tea leaves. Elizabeth's knitting them all rugs to keep them warm (and win brownie points now we're going to survive), Wilbur's teaching Kate how to play the didgeridoo, which she appears to have a natural face for, deaf Grandma and deaf Jack are fighting in the armchairs while we tow them along behind, and Edwin and Edwina are cooking up a storm of Chinese noodles and frozen meat pies.

8.49 pm PHEW!

It looks like we might just be all right. So whatever your name is, I want to say thank you, wherever you are on Paradise Island for helping me get through all this. Writing to you has been important to me. You've stopped me from going bonkers, you've improved my typing, and you've made me realise that I've got what it takes to become a great writer: brash opinions and a lot of neuroses. So thank you, cause you've really saved my life, you and Babette's expensive moisturiser.

If you ever do feel like writing I'd really appreciate it, or at least write and just let me know your name. I mean if I'm going to harbour a grudge against you for the rest of my life, it'd be good to know what to call you.

8.51 pm

We're turning round the palm tree, past Mrs Simpson's plaque and the place where the water tank should have been, past the glimpse of a rooftop temple on Edwin and Edwina's Chinese restaurant, past Mary's chimney which has survived the wet because it's moulded out of left over fruitcake, past where Dad was fried by the power lines and past the ruins of our old cubby.

And we're heading out towards the main road. It's dark and the lights are flickering. I'm sort of pretending to be scared but really I've never felt so safe.

It's just an excuse to snuggle up to my hero, yep you guessed it, Dwayne.

8.58 pm

We're going through the entrance gate now and we're sailing down the main road. I'm turning round with Dwayne to look back at this toilet we're leaving and I can see the name of the caravan park in an arch up in lights: strong, loud and clear it reads

WELCOME TO PARADISE ISLAND

Hey, wait a minute ...

THE END